Access My eLab

GRAMMAR
FOR ACADEMIC PURPOSES

STEVE
MARSHALL

ACCURACY AND SENTENCE
STRUCTURE

Ⓟ Pearson

GSE

TO REGISTER

❶ Go to **mybookshelf.pearsonerpi.com**

❷ Follow the instructions. When asked for your access code, please type the code provided underneath the blue sticker.

❸ To access **My eLab** at any time, go to http://mybookshelf.pearsonerpi.com. **Bookmark this page for quicker access.**

Access to My eLab is valid for 12 months from the date of registration.

Online digital content not available for this VPL item.

WARNING! This book CANNOT BE RETURNED if the access code has been uncovered.

Note: Once you have registered, you will need to join your online class. Ask your teacher to provide you with the class ID.

TEACHER Access Code

To obtain an access code for My eLab, please contact your Pearson ELT consultant.

 I 800 263-3678, ext. 2
pearsonerpi.com/help

W139517 (A39518)

STEVE
MARSHALL

GRAMMAR
FOR
ACADEMIC
PURPOSES

ACCURACY AND SENTENCE
STRUCTURE

Product Owner
Stephan Leduc

Managing Editor
Sharnee Chait

Editor
Patricia Hynes

Project Editor
Emily Harrison

Art Director
Hélène Cousineau

Graphic Design Manager
Estelle Cuillerier

Book Design
Benoit Pitre

Book Layout
Nathalie Giroux

Cover Design
Cyclone Design Communications

Dedication
I would like to dedicate this book to Jamie, Joey, and Miki.

The publisher wishes to thank the following people for their helpful comments and suggestions:

Jerry Block, Fraser International College
Jennifer Carioto, Algonquin College
Kristibeth Kelly Delgado, Fanshawe College
Michelle Duhaney, Seneca College
Glenda Fish, Trent University
Eldon Friesen, Brock University
Izabella Kojic-Sabo, University of Windsor Centre for English
  Language Development
Dagmar Kulikova, Seneca College
Jennifer Walsh Marr, University of British Columbia Vantage College
Darlene Murphy, University of Würzburg
Bobbi Reimann, Catholic University of Eichstätt-Ingolstadt
Cyndy Reimer, Douglas College
Daniel Riccardi, University of British Columbia Vantage College
Skye Skagfeld, Vancouver Island University

INTRODUCTION

Successful academic writing requires competence in many key skills. Writers may be active readers, successful critical thinkers, and have a strong awareness of academic vocabulary and style. However, to apply skills and knowledge effectively, it is necessary to write with grammatical accuracy and employ a broad range of sentence structures. This is where *Grammar for Academic Purposes* can help!

Grammar for Academic Purposes is made up of fourteen units, each covering a key grammar and sentence structure skill. Each unit includes a clear and detailed explanation of rules, carefully designed tasks involving identification and analysis, writing practice activities, and a concise summary.

Helpful Appendices

Two comprehensive appendices can be used for reference. Appendix 1 focuses on *Linking Words in Academic Writing*: conjunctive adverbs, coordinators, subordinators, correlative conjunctions, and other commonly used linking words and phrases. Technical terms are explained in easy-to-understand language, with examples that illustrate usage. Appendix 2 brings together *35 Common Mistakes to Avoid in Academic Writing*, making it a useful reference tool for planning and self-editing work.

Customized My eLab

Grammar for Academic Purposes comes with a customized My eLab, providing an extensive grammar and sentence structure diagnostic and consolidation activities for each unit. Activities are self-grading with instant feedback allowing students to work at their own pace. Correct answers are acknowledged. If an answer is wrong, a pop-up will explain why the answer is wrong and will indicate the page(s) in the unit where more detailed explanations can be found.

Who Is This Book For?

Grammar for Academic Purposes is suitable for students taking preparatory courses in English for Academic Purposes, IELTS, and TOEFL, or for those doing self-study, with the following minimum levels: IELTS 6.0   CEFR B2   Pearson GSE 78

This book is suitable for teachers looking for a comprehensive textbook that covers grammar and sentence structure in preparatory courses for English for Academic Purposes, IELTS, TOEFL, and academic writing.

Advance in Academic Writing

A version of *Grammar for Academic Purposes*, including the My eLab activities, is also available as an integrated Handbook with the purchase of the textbook or eText of *Advance in Academic Writing*, Pearson ELT.

Acknowledgements

I would like to thank the reviewers of *Advance in Academic Writing*, who provided comments and advice on an earlier version of this book. I also thank Patricia Hynes and Emily Harrison as well as Stephan Leduc and Sharnee Chait at Pearson ELT.

Steve Marshall, Vancouver, Canada

TABLE OF CONTENTS

UNIT 1 Tense and Aspect 1

UNIT 2 Articles, Nouns, and Noun Phrases 7

UNIT 3 Clauses and Sentences 15

UNIT 4 Relative Clauses 23

UNIT 5 Punctuation: Commas and Semicolons 29

UNIT 6 Participle Phrases 38

UNIT 7 The Passive Voice 44

UNIT 8 Punctuation: Colons and Apostrophes 50

UNIT 9 Sentence Fragments, Comma Splices, and Run-On Sentences 59

UNIT 10 Subject-Verb Agreement 65

UNIT 11 Conditional Sentences 71

UNIT 12 Parallel Structure 79

UNIT 13 Modal Auxiliary Verbs to Express Likelihood and Obligation 83

UNIT 14 Inversion for Emphasis 93

APPENDIX 1 Linking Words in Academic Writing 101

APPENDIX 2 35 Mistakes to Avoid in Academic Writing 110

GLOSSARY 121

TENSE AND ASPECT

What Is Tense?

We use different verb tenses to place actions and states in different time periods: past, present, and future. In the following examples, the verb is in bold and the expression of time, underlined:

I **am** in my third year at college <u>now</u>. (present simple tense for present time)

I **passed** all my courses <u>last term</u>. (past simple tense for past time)

I**'m going to graduate** <u>next year</u>. (future with *going to* for future time)

What Is Aspect?

Aspect refers to how actions and states relate to different time ideas. There are two kinds of aspect: perfect and continuous. Perfect aspect indicates a relationship between two time periods, for example, past and present, past and past, present and future, or future and future. Continuous aspect indicates that an action is, was, or will be in progress at a certain time.

Perfect Aspect

I**'ve lived** on campus <u>for two years</u>. (present perfect simple tense)

In the example above, the present perfect simple tense is used to explain a relationship between the past and the present. The speaker began living on campus two years ago and is still living there at the time of speaking. The perfect aspect in this sentence is the relationship between then and now—in this case, an unfinished period of time. The perfect aspect is formed with the auxiliary verb *have* followed by the past participle of the main verb: I*'ve lived*.

Continuous Aspect

I**'m studying** <u>now</u>. Please call later. (present continuous tense)

In the example above, the present continuous tense is used to explain that an action is in progress at the time of speaking. The speaker cannot talk now because he or she is busy studying. The continuous aspect is formed with the auxiliary verb *be* followed by the main verb + *ing*: I*'m studying*.

Perfect and Continuous Aspect Together

I**'ve been studying** <u>all day</u>. (present perfect continuous tense)
That's why I'm tired.

In the example above, the present perfect continuous tense is used to describe a continuous action in unfinished time. The studying is continuous, and the time

> Simple tenses are normally defined as tenses with no auxiliary verbs. However, the term *simple* is used in this book with perfect tenses (which do have auxiliary verbs) to differentiate them from continuous forms, for example, present perfect simple as opposed to present perfect continuous.

is unfinished (the day has not ended). The emphasis is on the present result of the continuous past action: "that's why I'm tired." This sentence has perfect and continuous aspect.

TASK 1

Read the sentences below and answer the concept questions that follow. Refer to the summary at the end of the unit if you need help answering the questions.

Talking about the Past

a) I've lived on campus for two years.

b) I've been living on campus for two years.

1. Is the time idea in sentences a) and b) finished or unfinished?

_____

2. Which sentence could give the impression that the speaker intends to stay there permanently?

_____

_____

_____

c) I used to spend hours in the library during my first year.

d) I used to live on campus during my first year.

e) I would spend hours in the library during my first year.

f) I would live on campus during my first year.

3. Which of sentences c) to f) is not correct when talking about past habits, and why?

_____

_____

4. If you change the time idea to present and future for sentence f), what is the concept?

_____

_____

_____

_____

Talking about the Present

g) This month, I'm working as a research assistant (RA).

h) Sorry, I can't talk. I'm doing my RA job in the lab now.

i) If only I had time to work as an RA and earn some money.

5. In which sentence does it seem that the speaker does not have a job as an RA?

_____

_____

6. In which sentence might the speaker have a job as an RA but might not be doing the job at the time of speaking?

_____

_____

7. In which sentence is the speaker definitely working as an RA at the moment of speaking?

_____

_____

Talking about the Future

j) Wow! You got an A on the mock exam. I don't think you're going to fail!

k) I think I'll get good grades this year.

8. Which of sentences j) and k) is a general prediction, and which is a prediction based on present evidence? What is the evidence?

_____

_____

_____

_____

l) I'm going to take four courses next term.

m) I'll help you with your lab report if you like.

9. Which of sentences l) and m) is an intention, and which is an offer?

_____

_____

10. When did the speaker in sentence l) make the decision to take four courses next term: at the time of speaking or before?

_____

_____

11. When did the speaker in sentence m) make the decision to help: at the time of speaking or before?

_____

_____

TASK 2

Look again at the example sentences in Task 1. <u>Underline</u> any examples you find of perfect aspect and <mark>highlight</mark> any examples of continuous aspect. You will need to underline *and* highlight examples that represent both perfect and continuous aspect.

TASK 3

Read the paragraph below and fill in the blanks with appropriate verb forms. Use the verbs in brackets. There may be more than one correct answer for some blanks.

I _____ [live] in Korea when I _____ [be] a young child; then my parents _____ [decide] to move the family to California. I _____ [watch] TV one afternoon when they _____ [tell] me, "We _____ [move] to the United States." I _____ [remember] the day we _____ [arrive] like it _____ [be] yesterday. We _____ [fly] for 13 hours when the plane _____ [touch down] at Los Angeles airport. I _____ [visit] several other countries before, but the United States _____ [be] different. I _____ [live] in Los Angeles for 10 years now. During these 10 years, we _____ [move] house three times. At the moment, I _____ [be] really busy because I _____ [prepare] for my Grade 12 exams. If only I _____ [have] more time! My next exam _____ [be] only one week away. I think I _____ [do] OK as I _____ [prepare] well for this one. In fact, I think I _____ [pass] all of my exams. Once I _____ [finish], I _____ [visit] Florida with my family to celebrate. We _____ [plan] the trip for months. Hopefully, this time next month, I _____ [lie] on Miami Beach, and in one year, I _____ [pass] all my first-year college exams. My childhood in Korea _____ [seem] so far off now. I _____ [remember] how I _____ [spend] hours playing with my cousins during the summer holidays. Now I _____ [spend] most of my time studying!

My Bookshelf > My eLab > Exercises > Unit 1

TASK 4

Write a paragraph about the following:

- your past experience studying English
- your present living conditions
- your future study plans

Use as many of the tenses and verb forms described in this unit as you can.

_____

_____

_____

_____

_____

_____

_____

_____

_____

_____

_____

_____

_____

_____

_____

SUMMARY TENSES: PRESENT, PAST, AND FUTURE TIME

Tense/Form	Example	Concept
Talking about the Present		
Present simple	a) I **study** every day. b) Phnom Penh **is** the capital of Cambodia. c) Nurses **have** a demanding job. d) I **agree** with you.	a) A habit b) A fact c) A general truth d) A state
Present continuous	a) I**'m studying** now. Please call later. b) I can't go tonight. I**'m studying** this week. c) You**'re** always **interrupting** me!	a) Ongoing activity, happening now b) Ongoing activity, maybe happening now c) A habit, often annoying
Past tense for unreal present	a) It's time you **studied** harder. b) If only I **had** more money.	a) You're not studying hard. (action verb) b) I don't have enough money. (state verb)

Tense/Form	Example	Concept
Talking about the Past		
Past simple	a) I **studied** too much last week. b) I **had** no time to relax.	a) Finished past, time idea stated b) Finished past, time idea understood
Past continuous	I **was studying** when you phoned me.	Action in progress at a specific past time
Present perfect simple	a) I'**ve lived** in Spain for 10 years. b) I'**ve attended** three different colleges. c) I'**ve passed** the exam!	a) Unfinished past: I still live there. b) Life experience c) One action, with focus on the present result: I'm happy!
Present perfect continuous	a) I'**ve been living** here for two years. b) Sorry I'm late. I'**ve been driving** for an hour. c) I'**ve been studying** all day.	a) Unfinished past: I still live here. (can seem temporary) b) Continued action, recently finished c) Continued action, with focus on the present result: I'm tired.
Past perfect simple	When I got to the station, the train **had** just **left**.	One past action happened before another.
Past perfect continuous	I **had been studying** all day when you arrived.	One continuous past action happened before another.
Used to for past habit	a) I **used to study** all day during exam time. b) I **used to have** a lot of free time at college.	a) I don't do it any more. (action verb) b) I don't have free time now. (state verb)
Would for past habit	I **would study** all day during the exam period.	I don't do it any more. (action verb) *Do not use *would* for past states.
Talking about the Future		
Future with *will*	a) I think you'**ll do** well on the exam. b) Don't worry. I'**ll check** your essay.	a) A general prediction b) An offer, a spontaneous decision
Future with *going to*	a) I think I'**m going to do** well on the exam. I just got an A on the practice paper. b) I'**m going to major** in Computer Science.	a) A prediction based on present evidence b) A future intention, decision made in the past
Present simple for future	The next class **begins** in 20 minutes.	Timetable future: it's scheduled.
Present continuous for future	I'**m staying** with my cousins next week.	Arranged future
Future continuous	This time tomorrow, I'**ll be taking** my English exam.	A temporary continuous action at a specific future time
Future perfect	This time next week, I'**ll have finished** all my exams.	An action finished before a specific future time
Future perfect continuous	I expect I'**ll have been studying** for 10 hours when you get here.	A continuous action finished before a specific future time

ARTICLES, NOUNS, AND NOUN PHRASES

When you describe things in English, you often have to use articles such as *a/an* and *the* in front of the noun.

> I need to borrow **a dictionary**.

> **The chairs in Room 3** are uncomfortable.

Other times, there is no article in front of the noun. Instead, the noun is in plural or uncountable form with no article.

> **Online dictionaries** are convenient.

> I love doing **research**.

You need to follow two stages to understand how to use articles correctly when forming noun phrases in English, and to understand how meanings can change with the different uses.

STAGE 1   GENERAL OR SPECIFIC?

The first question to ask when you use a noun phrase to describe something in English is the following: "Is the concept general or specific?"

General means that you are using a noun phrase to refer to all members of a group or category. For example, if you write "Online dictionaries are convenient," you are referring to all online dictionaries, that is, all members of the group "online dictionaries." This is a general noun phrase.

Specific means that you are referring to a specific thing, or specific things. If, for example, you write "The chairs in Room 3 are uncomfortable," you are referring to those specific chairs, the ones in Room 3, not all chairs. This is a specific noun phrase.

TASK 1

Indicate whether the noun or noun phrase in bold is general or specific.

		General	Specific
1	I often get lost in **libraries**.		
2	I often get lost in **the library**.		
3	You should drink **green tea** when you study.		
4	**The green tea I bought last week** is caffeine-free.		
5	I need to find **a roommate**.		
6	**The roommate I used to share with** has moved out.		

COUNTABLE OR UNCOUNTABLE?

The second question to ask when you use a noun phrase to describe something in English is the following: "Is the noun countable or uncountable?"

Countable Nouns

Countable nouns can be used in plural form and with the articles *a/an* and *the*.

> **Online dictionaries** are convenient.
>
> I need to borrow **a dictionary**.
>
> **The chairs in Room 3** are uncomfortable.

Uncountable Nouns

Uncountable nouns have no plural form. They can be used with or without the article *the*, but not with the article *a/an*.

> I love doing **research**.
>
> **The drinking water on campus** is filtered.

TASK 2

Indicate whether the noun or noun phrase in bold is countable or uncountable.

		Countable	Uncountable
1	I often get lost in **libraries**.		
2	I often get lost in **the library**.		
3	You should drink **green tea** when you study.		
4	**The green tea I bought last week** is caffeine-free.		
5	I need to find **a roommate**.		
6	**The roommate I used to share with** has moved out.		

NOUN PHRASES

How to Form General Noun Phrases

A general noun phrase refers to all members of a group. The rules for forming general noun phrases depend on whether the noun being described is countable or uncountable. Below you will learn three common types of general noun phrase (G1, G2, and G3) and one less common type (G4). (G stands for *general*.)

Remember this rule of thumb: you should not normally use *the* in general noun phrases.

G1. Use *a/an* + the singular noun.

> I need to borrow **a dictionary**.

This is general because *a dictionary* means *any* dictionary.

G2. Use the plural noun with no article.

Online dictionaries are convenient.

This is general because *online dictionaries* means *all* online dictionaries.

G3. Use an uncountable noun with no article.

I love doing **research**.

This is general because *research* means all types of research.

G4. Use *the* + the singular countable noun.

For species and inventions, and in academic analysis

> **G4a.** A recent study found **the black rhino** to be in critical danger of extinction.

> This is general because *the black rhino* means the species.

> **G4b. The digital textbook** has changed how students learn.

> This is general because *the digital textbook* means the invention. This form is also used with musical instruments, for example, *the piano*.

> **G4c. The Vice-President Research** leads research in most universities.

> This is general because *the Vice-President Research* means all VPRs when analyzing their role.

Note that the three sentences above could also be written using the G2 form and have exactly the same meaning:

> A recent study found **black rhinos** to be in critical danger of extinction.

> **Digital textbooks** have changed how students learn.

> **Vice-Presidents Research** lead research in most universities.

However, in academic writing, the G4 form can seem more formal and analytical than the G2 form.

How to Form Specific Noun Phrases

A specific noun phrase refers to a specific thing or things. The rules for forming specific noun phrases also relate to whether the noun being described is countable or uncountable. Below you will learn three common types of specific noun phrase (S1, S2, and S3) and one less common type (S4). (*S* stands for *specific*.)

Remember this rule of thumb: you should normally use *the* in specific noun phrases.

S1. Use *the* + the singular noun.

The projector in Room 3 isn't working.

This is specific because *the projector in Room 3* means the specific projector in that room.

S2. Use *the* + the plural noun.

The chairs in Room 3 are uncomfortable.

This is specific because *the chairs in Room 3* means the specific chairs in that room.

S3. Use *the* + the uncountable noun.

The drinking water on campus is filtered.

This is specific because *the drinking water on campus* refers specifically to the drinking water available on campus.

S4. Use *a/an* + the singular countable noun.

There is **a writing course** on Tuesdays.

This is specific because *a writing course* means a specific writing course being held on Tuesdays. When you introduce new information like this for the first time, use *a/an*. After the first mention, you should switch to *the* + the singular countable noun (S1):

The course starts next week.

It is clear from the context that *the course* is the same specific course—the writing course on Tuesdays.

TASK 3

Indicate whether the noun or noun phrase in bold is countable or uncountable, and general or specific. Then label each noun phrase according to the categories above, for example, G2 or S4. The first question has been done as an example. Refer to the summary at the end of the unit if necessary.

1. **Smart phones** can be used to help learning.

   ☑ countable ☐ uncountable ☑ general ☐ specific Type: _G2_

2. If students have **a smart phone**, they can access a lot of information.

   ☐ countable ☐ uncountable ☐ general ☐ specific Type: ____

3. After I bought **a smart phone**, I changed how I studied.

   ☐ countable ☐ uncountable ☐ general ☐ specific Type: ____

4. **The smart phone** has changed how students learn.

   ☐ countable ☐ uncountable ☐ general ☐ specific Type: ____

5. We're meeting in **the classroom next to the lab**.

   ☐ countable ☐ uncountable ☐ general ☐ specific Type: ____

6. **The classrooms in the South Campus** are equipped for video-conferencing.

   ☐ countable ☐ uncountable ☐ general ☐ specific Type: ____

7. **The classrooms** are also air-conditioned.

   ☐ countable ☐ uncountable ☐ general ☐ specific Type: ____

8. We donated **the money we collected last month** to a local children's charity.

☐ countable ☐ uncountable ☐ general ☐ specific Type: ____

9. **Money** can't solve every problem, but it can help.

☐ countable ☐ uncountable ☐ general ☐ specific Type: ____

Shared Knowledge in Specific Noun Phrases

When you use specific noun phrases, you share knowledge with your listener or reader. Shared knowledge can be *explicitly stated* or *implicitly understood* in specific noun phrases.

Explicitly stated means that the shared knowledge is included in the noun phrase in the form of specifying information so that the listener or reader can understand which specific thing you are describing. *Implicitly understood* means that the specifying information is not included in the noun phrase because it is not necessary: the listener or reader can understand which specific thing you are describing from the context.

The following examples from Task 3 illustrate this difference.

> **The classrooms <u>in the South Campus</u>** are equipped for video-conferencing. (shared knowledge explicitly stated)

The writer has added *in the South Campus* as specifying information to make it clear to the reader which classrooms are being described. Without this information, the reader would not understand the specific reference, i.e., which classrooms.

> **The classrooms** are also air-conditioned. (shared knowledge implicitly understood)

The writer has not added any specifying information because the context can be implicitly understood from the previous sentence. The reader understands that *the classrooms* refers to the classrooms in the South Campus, so it is not necessary to repeat this information. Where the context is clear and can be implicitly understood, writers (and speakers) tend to avoid specifying information.

TASK 4

Indicate whether the shared knowledge is stated explicitly or understood implicitly in the noun phrases in bold. <u>Underline</u> any specifying information.

		Explicit	Implicit
1	**The increase in college tuition fees** came into effect last month.		
2	**The increase** was not popular with the students.		
3	TEACHER: "Can someone pass by? **The video-conferencing machine** isn't working." TECHNICIAN: "Which one are you talking about?"		
4	TEACHER: "Oh, sorry. I meant **the video-conferencing machine in EDF25** isn't working." TECHNICIAN: "I'll send someone over to help you in the next 10 minutes."		

TASK 5

Read the following paragraph. The nouns and noun phrases in bold are incorrect. Fix the errors by writing the correct forms above the noun phrases. Then label each noun phrase according to the categories described on pages 8 to 10, for example, G2 or S4.

The Hubble Telescope

Telescope has revolutionized astronomy since its invention in the 17th century.

Since then, **the astronomers** have spent years studying the universe through tele-

scopic lenses. In 1990, **large telescope** was sent into orbit to study the universe:

the Hubble Telescope. **Telescope** was named Hubble after the astronomer Edwin

Hubble. The images it has sent back to Earth have given us new insight into **star**

and planet in our galaxy. Anyone can use **personal computer** to look at its images

via the Internet. Anyone wanting to do **the research** can apply to use the Hubble

Telescope. If someone sends a research proposal, a panel of leading astronomers

will review **research** and its potential impact on **field of astronomy**.

My Bookshelf > My eLab >
Exercises > Unit 2

TASK 6

Read the excerpts below from the introduction (titled "Background") to the following article: Beghi, G. M., & Morselli-Labate, A. M. (2016). Does homeopathic medicine have a preventive effect on respiratory tract infections? A real life observational study. Multidisciplinary respiratory medicine, 11(1), 12.

Selected noun phrases are in bold. Analyze how and why the authors use general and specific noun phrases in this section. Label the noun phrases *G* for general or *S* for specific in the left margin. Do you notice any patterns of usage?

Background

[1] **Integrative medicine** (IM) refers to all those treatments that are not part of **conventional healthcare**. **Homeopathy** is a system of IM that was developed in Europe at the end of the eighteenth century employing **medicines** prepared according to a well-defined procedure starting from mineral, herbal or animal substances. ...

[2] According to the 2012 National Health Interview Survey (NHIS) approximately 5 million adults and 1 million children in the United States used **homeopathy** in 2011. According to the 2014 Italian National Institute of Statistics (ISTAT)

survey, **homeopathic products** have been used by approximately 2.5 million people in Italy in the years 2010–2013 and they have been prescribed by over 20,000 physicians. ...

[3] **An observational longitudinal study conducted in Italy between 1998 and 2008** analysed **the socio-demographic features** and **the outcomes of a paediatric population treated with homeopathic medicine. The results** were promising and indicated **a positive therapeutic response**, especially in children affected by respiratory diseases (Rossi et al., 2010). ...

[4] This paper presents **the results of a retrospective controlled observational study** designed to examine health changes, expressed as **the reduction in the average number of RTI episodes per year**, of a cohort of patients undergoing homeopathic treatment versus **a control group of untreated patients**, in a real-world setting.

Patterns of usage: _____

_____

_____

_____

TASK 7

Write four sentences containing general or specific noun phrases. In each sentence, use at least two nouns from each of the following lists of vocabulary related to experimental research.

Countable Nouns
- control group
- double-blind control trial
- experiment
- expert
- participant
- patient
- result

Uncountable Nouns
- bias
- homeopathy
- medicine
- placebo effect
- popularity
- research

1. _____

_____

2. _____

_____

3. _____

_____

4. _____

_____

	Category: General or Specific? Countable or Uncountable?		Form	Example	Concept
G1	General	Countable	*a/an* + singular noun	I need to borrow **a dictionary**.	Any dictionary
G2	General	Countable	Plural noun (no article)	**Online dictionaries** are convenient.	All online dictionaries
G3	General	Uncountable	Uncountable noun (no article)	I love doing **research**.	All types of research
G4	General	Countable	*the* + singular noun	a) **The black rhino** is in critical danger of extinction. b) **The digital textbook** has changed how students learn. c) **The Vice-President Research (VPR)** leads research in most universities.	a) The species: all black rhinos b) The invention: all digital textbooks c) All VPRs (analysis of their role)
S1	Specific	Countable	*the* + singular noun	**The projector in Room 3** isn't working.	The specific projector in that room
S2	Specific	Countable	*the* + plural noun	**The chairs in Room 3** are uncomfortable.	The specific chairs in that room
S3	Specific	Uncountable	*the* + uncountable noun	**The drinking water on campus** is filtered.	Specifically, the drinking water available on campus
S4	Specific	Countable	*a/an* + singular noun	There is **a writing course** on Tuesdays. *****The course** starts next week.	New information: first mention *After the first mention, use *the* + singular noun (S1).

Shared Knowledge in Specific Noun Phrases	Example		Concept
Explicitly stated	**The projector in Room 3** isn't working.		The specifying information *in Room 3* makes it clear which projector.
Implicitly understood	Can someone come and fix **the projector**?		No specifying information: the previous sentence makes it clear which projector.

CLAUSES AND SENTENCES

| CLAUSES | **TWO TYPES OF CLAUSES** |

What Is a Clause?

A clause can be defined as follows:

- a group of words that forms a whole sentence, or part of a sentence
- a group of words that has a subject and a corresponding verb
- different from a phrase, which does not have a subject and a verb

Clauses versus Phrases

Examples of Clauses

In the following examples, the subject of the clause is in bold and the verb, underlined.

The road works <u>led</u> to traffic congestion.   (independent clause – stands alone as a sentence)

which <u>led</u> to traffic congestion   (dependent clause – cannot stand alone as a sentence)

The city <u>introduced</u> road pricing.   (independent clause – stands alone as a sentence)

Although **the city** <u>introduced</u> road pricing,   (dependent clause – cannot stand alone as a sentence)

Examples of Phrases

with so much traffic congestion   (preposition phrase – lacks a subject and verb)

the introduction of road pricing   (noun phrase – lacks a subject and verb)

bringing benefits to local communities   (participle phrase – lacks a subject and corresponding verb)

Learn more about participle phrases in Unit 6, p. 38.

Knowing the difference between an independent and a dependent clause will help you improve your sentence structure and punctuation, and make your writing more cohesive.

TASK 1

Indicate whether the underlined words in each sentence form a clause or a phrase.

		Clause	Phrase
1	<u>Because of road pricing</u>, rush-hour congestion fell.		
2	Traffic pollution went down <u>in the following months</u>.		
3	<u>Although pollution went down</u>, car traffic remained the same.		
4	Although pollution went down, <u>car traffic remained the same</u>.		
5	Pollution fell, <u>benefiting local communities</u>.		
6	<u>Introduced last year</u>, road pricing has reduced pollution.		

What Is an Independent Clause?

As stated above, an independent clause has a subject and a corresponding verb. An independent clause can stand alone as a sentence, expressing a complete thought or idea. Independent clauses are also called *main* clauses.

Below are the two independent clauses from the preceding section. The subjects are in bold and the verbs, underlined.

1. **The road works** <u>led</u> to traffic congestion.

2. **The city** <u>introduced</u> road pricing.

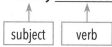

Examples 1 and 2 are both complete sentences. Each has a subject and a corresponding verb. When an independent clause forms a complete sentence, it is called a *simple* sentence.

However, independent clauses often form part of a sentence rather than the whole sentence, as illustrated below. The independent clauses are underlined; the dependent clause is in italics.

1. <u>The city introduced road pricing</u>, and <u>rush-hour congestion fell</u>.

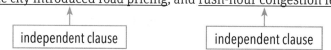

2. <u>The road works led to traffic congestion</u>, *which increased pollution in the area.*

Sentence 1 contains two independent clauses, joined by the coordinator *and*. This is called a *compound* sentence. Sentence 2 contains one independent clause and one dependent clause. Together, they form a *complex* sentence.

What Is a Dependent Clause?

A dependent clause is called *dependent* because it cannot stand alone as a sentence. Nor does it express a complete thought or idea. Dependent clauses are also called *subordinate* clauses. As clauses, they have a subject (or a word that functions grammatically as a subject) and a corresponding verb.

Below are the two dependent clauses from the first page of this unit. The keywords that make them dependent are in bold.

1. **which** led to traffic congestion
2. **Although** the city introduced road pricing,

Learn more about relative clauses in Unit 4, p. 23.

Example 1 begins with the relative pronoun *which*. This makes the clause dependent. Other relative pronouns are *that*, *who*, *when*, *where*, *why*, and *what*.

Learn more about subordinators as linking words in Appendix 1, p. 107.

Example 2 begins with the subordinator *although*, making the clause dependent. Many other subordinators make clauses dependent in this way, for example, *while*, *because*, and *unless*.

Examples 1 and 2 do not express whole thoughts or ideas. The following are two ways to make the thought or idea whole and the sentences complete:

1. Join the dependent clause to an independent clause.

The road works lasted two weeks, *which led to traffic congestion.*   (complex sentence)

Although the city introduced road pricing, traffic congestion remained a problem.   (complex sentence)

2. Replace or remove the relative pronoun or the subordinator.

~~which~~ The road works led to traffic congestion.

~~Although~~ The city introduced road pricing.

With the above changes, each dependent clause has become a complete sentence that expresses a whole idea. If written as sentences, without these changes, the dependent clauses would be *sentence fragments*, or incomplete sentences, as illustrated below:

Learn more about sentence fragments in Unit 9, p. 59.

Which led to traffic congestion.   (sentence fragment)

Although the city introduced road pricing.   (sentence fragment)

TASK 2

Indicate whether the underlined words in each sentence form an independent or a dependent clause.

		Independent	Dependent
1	Due to the introduction of road pricing, <u>there was a reduction in rush-hour traffic</u>.		
2	<u>Traffic pollution went down</u> in the following months.		
3	<u>While rush-hour traffic fell</u>, the number of road accidents remained the same.		
4	<u>The number of accidents did not go down</u>.		
5	The accident rate increased on bridges, <u>where more drivers were speeding</u>.		

Simple Sentences

When an independent clause forms a complete sentence, it is called a *simple* sentence. Below are two examples from the preceding section on clauses. Each expresses one whole thought or idea. A simple sentence must contain a subject and a corresponding verb.

1. **The road works** <u>led</u> to traffic congestion.

   subject | verb

2. **The city** <u>introduced</u> road pricing.

   subject | verb

Compound Sentences

When two independent clauses are joined together in a sentence by one of the "FANBOYS" coordinators (*for*, *and*, *nor*, *but*, *or*, *yet*, *so*), the sentence is called a *compound* sentence. Consider the example below, with the independent clauses underlined and the coordinator, in bold. The compound sentence expresses two whole thoughts or ideas and gives equal emphasis to each of them.

<u>The city introduced road pricing</u>, **and** <u>rush-hour congestion fell</u>.

independent clause   independent clause

Complex Sentences

When a dependent clause and an independent clause are combined in one sentence, the sentence is called a *complex* sentence. Consider the example below, with the independent clause underlined and the dependent clause, in italics. In this sentence, the independent clause comes second and carries more emphasis than the dependent clause. The question in parentheses illustrates the idea of emphasis.

Although the city introduced cycle lanes,   (How can we solve the problem?)
<u>pollution remained a problem</u>.

TASK 3

Identify the sentences below as simple, compound, or complex.

1. The number of accidents fell.
   ☐ simple   ☐ compound   ☐ complex

2. Traffic pollution went down in the following months.
   ☐ simple   ☐ compound   ☐ complex

3. Although rush hour was less busy, overall traffic rates did not fall.
   ☐ simple   ☐ compound   ☐ complex

4. The local government gained revenue, but drivers were not happy.

☐ simple ☐ compound ☐ complex

5. The policy was unpopular with drivers who lived in the suburbs.

☐ simple ☐ compound ☐ complex

6. The number of accidents fell, and government revenue increased.

☐ simple ☐ compound ☐ complex

Emphasizing Information with Sentence Structure

Speakers often use intonation to give emphasis to words or phrases. In written English, sentence structure can also be used to emphasize information. In compound sentences, the ideas in the clauses are given equal weight, while in complex sentences, the idea in the independent clause often carries more emphasis when it comes at the end of the sentence.

TASK 4

1. Read the sentences below, which relate to the introduction of bicycle lanes to improve safety for cyclists. Indicate whether two ideas are given equal emphasis or whether one is emphasized over the other. If one idea is emphasized, <u>underline</u> the clause that expresses that idea.

		Equal Emphasis	One Idea Emphasized
a)	The number of cyclists rose, and the accident rate fell.		
b)	As cyclists were better protected, the number of accidents fell.		
c)	Cycling became safer, but traffic remained the same.		
d)	Although cycling became safer, traffic remained the same.		

Note that when the dependent clause comes after the independent clause, as in b), no comma separates the two.

2. Now compare the two sentences below. In Sentence a), the dependent clause comes before the independent clause. In sentence b), the dependent clause comes after the independent clause.

a) As cyclists were better protected, the number of accidents fell.

b) The number of accidents fell as cyclists were better protected.

How does changing the order of the clauses in sentence b) affect your interpretation of emphasis?

_____

_____

_____

_____

_____

_____

_____

My Bookshelf > My eLab >
Exercises > Unit 3

Sentence Types: Getting the Right Balance

It is important to use a range of sentence types in academic writing. If you write with a balance of different sentence types, it adds variety to your writing and makes it more engaging and readable. However, the decision about which type of sentence to use cannot be random: it depends on several factors, including how you want to add emphasis.

The following are factors to consider when choosing sentence types:

- The clauses in compound sentences often carry equal emphasis.

  The city introduced road pricing, and rush-hour congestion fell.

- Complex sentences often give emphasis to the idea in the independent clause when it comes at the end of the sentence. In the following example, the independent clause, *pollution remained a problem*, receives more emphasis.

  Although the city introduced cycle lanes, pollution remained a problem.

- Avoid choppy writing: too many simple sentences make it difficult to read the text and link the ideas.

  The city introduced road pricing last year. Consequently, the number of rush-hour drivers fell. Moreover, the accident rate fell. The local government was pleased with the revenue raised. However, the overall number of car journeys stayed the same.

- Find alternatives to compound sentences to describe complex relationships between ideas.

  1. The city introduced road pricing last year, and rush-hour congestion fell.

  2. After the city introduced road pricing last year, rush-hour congestion fell.

  3. The city introduced road pricing last year, which led to a fall in rush-hour congestion.

  4. The city introduced road pricing last year. As a result, rush-hour congestion fell.

Compound sentence 1 is acceptable but lacks precision. Complex sentences 2 and 3 are more precise, as is example 4: two simple sentences linked by a conjunctive adverb.

TASK 5

The paragraph below contains too many simple sentences. As a result, the writing is repetitive and lacks flow. Rewrite the paragraph, forming compound and complex sentences as appropriate. You do not need to change every simple sentence.

Road Safety

Road safety is an important issue in all cities. There are too many accidents on the roads of our cities today. These accidents are mostly caused by unsafe driving. The police need to be stricter. Cyclists and pedestrians need to take more responsibility on the roads. Safe driving is the main solution. Stricter policing may work; improved driver education may provide the best solution.

_____

_____

_____

_____

_____

_____

TASK 6

The paragraph below contains too many compound sentences. (Note the coordinators in bold.) As a result, the writing seems simplistic in places, lacking precision and emphasis where needed. Rewrite the paragraph, forming complex and simple sentences as appropriate. You do not need to change every compound sentence.

Air Travel

Many more people travel by air than 30 years ago, **but** air travel remains too expensive for a large percentage of the world's population. In large developed countries such as Canada, the United States, and Australia, cities are far apart, **and** air travel is often the only option for travellers. Cities are connected by roads, **but** the distances and harsh climates make driving very difficult, time-consuming, and expensive. Airfares have fallen significantly in the last 15 years, **so** many more people can now afford to fly.

_____

_____

_____

_____

_____

_____

Type	Examples	Concept/Form
Clauses		
Independent	The city introduced road pricing.	• One whole idea • Can stand alone as a sentence • Has a subject and a corresponding verb
Dependent	… which led to traffic congestion Although the city introduced cycle lanes,	• Not a whole idea • Cannot stand alone as a sentence • Commonly formed with a subordinator or a relative pronoun • Has a verb that corresponds with a subject
Sentences		
Simple	The city introduced cycle lanes.	• One whole idea • One independent clause
Compound	The city introduced cycle lanes, but the congestion continued.	• Two or more ideas with equal emphasis • Two or more independent clauses joined by a coordinator, or coordinators
Complex	The accident rate fell, which pleased cyclists. Although cycling became safer, car traffic remained the same.	• Two or more ideas, with one given greater emphasis • Emphasis often on the idea in independent clause • One or more independent clauses combined with one or more dependent clauses, in variable order

RELATIVE CLAUSES

What Is a Relative Clause?

Relative clauses give defining or additional information about an important idea or thing in an independent clause. There are two kinds of relative clauses: defining and non-defining (also referred to as *restrictive* and *non-restrictive* clauses). Relative clauses can begin with any of the following relative pronouns (the context in which they are used is in parentheses):

- *which* (a thing)
- *that* (a thing or person)
- *who(m)* (a person)
- *whose* (possessive form)
- *what* (the thing that)
- *when* (time)
- *where* (place)
- *why* (reason)

Defining Relative Clauses

A defining relative clause defines, or identifies, an important thing or idea in an independent clause. Defining relative clauses provide information that is essential for the reader to understand the sentence.

> The computer *that I bought yesterday* was really expensive.

In the example sentence, the independent clause is *The computer was really expensive*. The defining relative clause is *that I bought yesterday*.

Essential Information

The defining relative clause is essential because it identifies the specific computer that the writer is describing. Without this information, the meaning of the sentence would not be clear or complete.

That or *Which*?

In defining relative clauses that describe things, it is possible to use *that* or *which* as the relative pronoun. It is more common to use *that*, especially in North American English. *Which* is more commonly used in British English:

> The computer ***which*** *I bought yesterday* was really expensive.

Commas

Defining relative clauses are not set off with commas.

Non-Defining Relative Clauses

A non-defining relative clause gives extra, non-essential information about an important thing or idea in an independent clause.

> My new computer, *which has high-resolution display*, was really expensive.

In the example sentence, the independent clause is *My new computer was really expensive*. The non-defining relative clause is *which has high-resolution display*.

Non-defining relative clauses can refer to something specific in the independent clause or to the general idea, as the following examples illustrate:

My new computer, *which has high-resolution display*, was really expensive.	(extra information about the computer—a specific thing)
I spilled coffee on my new computer, *which was really careless of me*.	(extra information about spilling coffee on my computer—the general idea)

Non-Essential Information

The non-defining relative clause is not essential because it gives extra, incidental information. Without the non-defining relative clause, the meaning of the sentence would still be clear and complete.

That or *Which?*

In non-defining relative clauses that describe things, it is not possible to use *that*; *which* is the only correct choice:

> *which*
> My new computer, ~~*that*~~ has high-resolution display, was really expensive.

Commas

Non-defining relative clauses must be set off with commas.

Relative Pronouns

In addition to *that* and *which*, several different relative pronouns are commonly used in defining and non-defining relative clauses:

- *who(m)* (a person)

  1. Subject relative clause

  ✓ She's the teacher **who/that** *taught me last year*.

  ✗ She's the teacher **whom** *taught me last year*.

  Do not use *whom*, because the pronoun (referring to *the teacher*) is the subject of the relative clause: **She** *taught me*.

  2. Object relative clause

  She's the teacher **who/that** *I recommended to you*.

  She's the teacher **whom** *I recommended to you*. (more formal)

  You can use *whom* because the pronoun (referring to *the teacher*) is the object of the relative clause: *I recommended* **her** *to you*.

> You can use *that* for people although this usage is often considered informal and more appropriate in spoken English.

> Often speakers omit the relative pronoun in sentences, e.g., *She's the teacher I recommended to you*. See the section on this topic on page 26.

- *whose* (possessive form)

  That teacher, **whose** *name I can't remember*, taught me last term.

  Whose is used mostly for people, as above, and animals; however, it can also be used for inanimate objects. This second use is grammatically possible but less common:

  The library, **whose** *collection exceeds one million books*, is the largest in the city.

- *what* (the thing that)

  I can't decide **what** *I should write for the assignment*.

- *when* (time)

  The early evening is **when** *I can study best*.

- *where* (place)

  This is the room **where** *we took a class last year*.

- *why* (reason)

  The teaching assistant explained to me **why** *I got a B grade*.

Relative Clauses Containing Prepositions

There are two ways to write relative clauses containing prepositions: with the preposition at the beginning or at the end of the relative clause.

1. **That**'s the class that everyone was talking **about**.
2. **That**'s the class **about which** everyone was talking. (Do not write *about that*.)
3. He's the friend **who** *I went to school* **with**.
4. He's the friend **with whom** *I went to school*. (Do not write *with who*.)

In examples 1 and 3, the sentences end with a preposition. This is informal, conversational style. In examples 2 and 4, the relative clauses begin with the prepositions *about* and *with*. This is formal style that is appropriate for academic writing. It is common practice to avoid ending sentences with prepositions in academic writing unless the alternative form seems overly formal or awkward.

TASK 1

Indicate whether the relative clauses (in italics) in the following sentences are defining or non-defining.

		Defining	Non-Defining
1	I got an A for the Economics class *that I took last term*.		
2	Let's meet in the computer room *where we studied last time*.		
3	The Economics class, *which was at the South Campus*, was really difficult.		
4	I did the project with a friend *who I went to school with*.		
5	I did the project with my school friend, *who was really helpful*.		
6	I did the project with my school friend, *which was lots of fun*.		

Omitting the Relative Pronoun in Defining Relative Clauses

It is not always necessary to include the relative pronoun in a defining relative clause, depending on whether the clause is a subject or object relative clause.

Subject Relative Clause

✓ I learned a lot from the instructor **who** taught Economics last term.

✗ I learned a lot from the instructor taught Economics last term.

In the example above, the relative clause is *who taught Economics last term*. It is a defining clause because it gives essential information about the instructor, explaining *which* instructor and thus making the idea of the sentence complete. The relative pronoun *who* cannot be omitted because it is part of a subject-defining relative clause: the person being defined, the instructor, is the subject of the defining relative clause:

The instructor taught Economics last term.

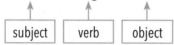

| subject | verb | object |

Object Relative Clause

1. I got an A for the Economics class **that** I took last term.
2. I got an A for the Economics class I took last term.

In sentence 1, the relative clause is *that I took last term*. It is a defining clause because it gives essential information about the Economics class to make the idea of the sentence complete. In sentence 2, the relative pronoun *that* can be omitted because it is part of an object-defining relative clause: the thing being defined, the Economics class, is the object of the defining relative clause:

I took the Economics class last term.

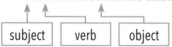

| subject | verb | object |

TASK 2

In the defining relative clauses below, all of the relative pronouns are included. <u>Underline</u> the relative clause, and decide whether the person or thing being defined is the subject or object of the relative clause. Then state whether the relative pronoun can be omitted.

		Subject or Object?	Omit Pronoun?
1	The class that I was trying to take was full.		
2	The course that I'm most excited about is Kinesiology.		
3	The course that interests me most is Kinesiology.		
4	The class that was the most difficult was Economics 101.		
5	The class that I studied hardest for was Economics 101.		

TASK 3

Complete the defining and non-defining relative clauses in the following sentences. If the sentence requires an object-defining relative clause, omit the relative pronoun.

1. Last week I finished my final assignment, which _____.

2. He's the friend _____ talking about yesterday.

3. Your hard work is _____ admire most about you.

4. She's the professor _____ the national award.

5. He's the professor whose _____.

6. She's the professor _____ told you about.

7. She's the professor about _____.

8. Professor Lee, _____ class I took last year, is really helpful.

9. Professor Lee, _____ won the award, is really helpful.

10. I'm looking for a place _____ study quietly.

11. I'm looking for a room _____ study quietly in.

My Bookshelf > My eLab >
Exercises > Unit 4

TASK 4

Write a paragraph of at least six sentences on the topic of "looking back." Each sentence should relate to one of the prompts below and include a relative clause. Try to link the sentences together coherently and cohesively.

1. A thing that you will always remember
2. A thing that you still enjoy today
3. A teacher who had a major influence on you
4. A time when you were under pressure to succeed
5. A place where you felt relaxed
6. The reason why you are studying your current subject
7. A teacher whose class you took
8. A person with whom you got along well

RELATIVE CLAUSES

	Examples	Concept/Form
Types of Relative Clause		
Defining	The Business class *that I'm taking* is difficult.	• Essential information about something important in the independent clause • No commas • Use *that*. • Also possible to use *which* in British English
Non-defining	The Business class, *which is really difficult*, is on Tuesday afternoons. (refers to the class) I got an A in Business, *which surprised me*! (refers to the general idea: getting an A)	• Non-essential information about something important in the independent clause or about the general idea of the clause • Set off with commas • Do not use *that*.
Relative Pronouns		
that and *which*	The computer **that/which** *I bought yesterday* was expensive.	• A thing
who and *whom*	She's the teacher **who** *taught me last year*. She's the teacher **whom** *I recommended to you*.	• A person • Also possible to use *that* • Use *whom* for object relative clauses: I recommended **her** to you.
whose	She's the teacher **whose** *class I took last year*.	Possessive form: I took **her** class.
what	I can't decide **what** *I should write for the assignment*.	The thing that
when	Let's meet in the evening, **when** *it's quieter*.	The time
where	This is the room **where** *we took a class last year*.	The place
why	The TA wouldn't tell me **why** *I got a B grade*.	The reason
Omitting the Pronoun in Defining Relative Clauses		
Subject-defining relative clause	I like the instructor **who** *taught Chemistry 199 last term*.	• **The instructor** is the subject of the relative clause. • Impossible to omit the pronoun
Object-defining relative clause	I got a B+ for the Chemistry class **that** *I took last term*. I got a B+ for the Chemistry class *I took last term*.	• **the Chemistry class** is the object of the relative clause. • Possible to omit the pronoun
Relative Clauses Containing Prepositions		
Preposition at the end of the clause	***That***'s the class that everyone was talking **about**. He's the friend **who** *I went to school* **with**.	• Rule: Place preposition at the end of the clause. • Style: Informal and conversational
Preposition at the beginning of the clause	***That***'s the class **about** which everyone was talking. He's the friend **with whom** *I went to school*.	• Rule: *For that* or *with who* is incorrect. • Style: Formal, appropriate for academic writing (unless awkward)

PUNCTUATION: COMMAS AND SEMICOLONS

COMMAS ## THREE USES OF COMMAS

Commas are mostly used in two ways: to set off non-defining information in an independent clause, and before coordinating linking words such as *and*, *but*, and *so*. Another, less common use is to separate two or more adjectives before a noun. These rules for using commas are not always applied consistently by writers.

Adding Extra, Information to an Independent Clause

Before the Independent Clause

> Note that some writers do not consistently use commas before independent clauses, especially in journalistic writing.

- Preposition phrases:

  Since the 1970s, there has been a mandatory life sentence for murder in Canada.

  After the change of law, many judges complained about government interference.

  Across the country, the crime rate has fallen.

  With the fall in crime, many people felt safer.

  In universities and colleges, criminology students are studying why crime has fallen.

- Conjunctive adverbs:

  However, not all types of crime have fallen continuously. Online fraud is one example.

  Moreover, financially motivated crimes such as theft and burglary tend to rise during economic slowdowns.

  Therefore, social and economic factors should be considered when reading crime statistics.

- Dependent clauses:

  While violent crime fell, financially motivated crime rates fluctuated.

  If unemployment rates drop, violent crime rates also fall.

  Although there is a link between crime and poverty, other factors need to be considered.

- Participle phrases:

  Sensing a change in public opinion, the government unsuccessfully attempted to reinstate capital punishment in 1987.

  Influenced by recent opinion polls, the government unsuccessfully attempted to reinstate capital punishment in 1987.

Within the Independent Clause

- Conjunctive adverbs:

Not all types of crimes, **however,** have fallen continuously.

Social and economic factors should be considered, **therefore,** when reading crime statistics.

- Non-defining relative clauses:

The death penalty, **which is also known as *capital punishment*,** was abolished in Canada in 1976.

After 1976, convicted murderers, **who might previously have received the death penalty,** would receive mandatory life sentences instead.

- Non-defining participle phrases:

The death penalty, **also known as *capital punishment*,** was abolished in Canada in 1976.

In 1987, the government, **sensing a change in public opinion,** unsuccessfully attempted to reinstate capital punishment.

- Non-defining noun phrases:

Youth unemployment, **a root cause of financially motivated crimes,** has gone up in the current economic slowdown.

Rates for burglary and car theft, **two of the most common financially motivated crimes,** have increased significantly.

After the Independent Clause

- Conjunctive adverbs:

Financially motivated crimes such as theft and burglary tend to rise during economic slowdowns, **moreover**.

Not all types of crimes have fallen continuously, **however**.

- Non-defining relative clauses:

Criminologists have studied the death penalty and deterrence, **which is its ability to prevent other crimes**.

After 1976, mandatory life sentences applied for all convicted murderers, **which reflected the public mood.**

- Non-defining participle phrases:

Criminologists often study the pros and cons of the death penalty, **also known as *capital punishment***.

In 1987, the government tried to change the law, **sensing a change in public opinion**.

- Non-defining noun phrases:

The economic slowdown has led to increased youth unemployment, **a root cause of financially motivated crimes**.

The police are targeting burglary and car theft, **two of the most common financially motivated crimes**.

Coordination

To review compound sentences, see Unit 3, p. 18.

Before the "FANBOYS" Coordinators in Compound Sentences

Compound sentences are made up of two independent clauses joined by a coordinator (*for, and, nor, but, or, yet, so*).

- *and*

  Violent crime rates fell**, and** society became a lot safer.

- *but*

  Violent crime rates fell**, but** those for online fraud rose.

- *so*

  Mandatory life sentencing was introduced for murder**, so** the judiciary lost some of its independence.

Between the Items in Lists of Three or More Things

Stricter environments in some UK young offender institutions have resulted in inmates' [1] <u>having to wear uniforms</u>**,** [2] <u>being denied reading materials</u>**, and** [3] <u>ending their days at 10:30 p.m.</u>

No comma is required when only two things are joined by a coordinator:

Stricter environments in some UK young offender institutions have resulted in inmates' [1] <u>having to wear uniforms</u> **and** [2] <u>being denied reading materials</u>.

Separating Adjectives

Use commas to separate two or more adjectives belonging to the same category (e.g., opinion, shape, colour, material) when they come before the noun they describe:

Prisoners are now expected to live in a **harsher, more punitive** environment.

BUT

The local prison is a **big grey stone** building.

Variations on How to Use Commas

There are some variations on how to use commas that depend on the following factors.

British English

In British English, it is common to omit commas before coordinators such as *and, but,* and *so,* both in compound sentences and in lists of three or more things.

Violent crime rates fell with the increased police presence **and** the city became considerably safer in the months that followed.

Stricter environments in some UK young offender institutions have resulted in inmates' <u>having to wear uniforms</u>, <u>being denied reading materials</u> **and** <u>ending their days at 10:30 p.m.</u>

Journalistic Style

In journalistic style, commas are often omitted after introductory preposition phrases.

Since the 1970s there has been a mandatory life sentence for murder in Canada.

With the fall in crime many people felt safer.

To Avoid Confusion

Writers who usually omit commas (in British English and journalism, for example) sometimes have no choice but to include them to avoid confusing their readers. Consider the following examples:

1. With the fall in crime prevention became more of a focus than punishment.
2. With the fall in crime, prevention became more of a focus than punishment.

Sentence 1 would likely confuse the reader. This is because *crime prevention* is a common compound noun used in the discussion of crime. Without the comma, the reader might at first understand the sentence to be about "the fall in crime prevention." Readers often have to go back over such sentences two or three times to understand them. Sentence 2 is not confusing because there is a comma after the introductory phrase.

Sometimes writers add commas for clarity, to make it easier for the reader to process ideas or items in a list when confusion might arise. For example, although a comma is not needed before a coordinator joining two items, writers may include one to make the sentence more comprehensible.

1. Harsher environments in some prisons mean inmates receive fewer comforts that would make their stay in prison more tolerable and comfortable and stricter punishments if they break any of the rules of prison life.
2. Harsher environments in some prisons mean inmates receive <u>fewer comforts that would make their stay in prison more tolerable and comfortable</u>, and <u>stricter punishments if they break any of the rules of prison life</u>.

Sentence 1 could confuse the reader because the first item is *fewer comforts that would make their stay in prison more tolerable and comfortable*. Without the comma, the reader may think that the word *comfortable* is the beginning of the second item because it comes after the coordinator *and*. By placing the comma after the word *comfortable* in sentence 2, the writer avoids any confusion.

Personal Preference

Comma usage can also depend on the writer's personal style preferences. Writers may prefer not to use commas in some sentences if they feel it breaks the flow of the writing.

Remember: it is important to be consistent. For example, if you include a comma before the coordinator and in one sentence, make sure not to omit it in other sentences.

TASK 1

In the following sentences, there are no commas. Add commas where required. Some sentences may require more than one comma; others may require none. Then identify each comma according to its function: adding information to an independent clause (AI), coordination (C), or separation of adjectives (S).

Type of Comma

1. Although there is a link between alcohol consumption and crime other factors need to be considered. _____

2. During the last 30 years there has been a steady fall in crime rates in Canada. _____

3. There has nonetheless been an increase in cybercrimes. _____

4. Mandatory sentencing for the most violent crimes which takes some power away from judges has been popular with some members of the public but many judges disapprove. _____

5. Criminals who commit serious crimes in Sweden serve their sentences in a prison system that focuses on rehabilitation. _____

6. Aristotle said that poverty is the parent of crime which suggests a clear link between socio-economic factors and crime rates. _____

7. Violent crime rates have fallen across the country yet people still feel unsafe in some areas. _____

8. Crime policies aim for a safer more productive society. _____

9. The increased police presence aims to reassure people living in poor areas of the city. _____

TASK 2

The two sentences below could confuse readers. Explain why the sentences are confusing, and add commas to make them clearer.

1. After the mayor's promise to get tough on crime policies were implemented at the local level.

   _____

   _____

2. Due to the municipal government's measures to improve facilities for at-risk youth clubs for sport and learning were set up in three areas of the city.

   _____

   _____

TWO USES OF SEMICOLONS

Semicolons are used like periods to separate two independent clauses. Periods separate sentences; semicolons separate independent clauses in a sentence. Semicolons are also used to separate items in lists.

Separating Independent Clauses in a Sentence

Use semicolons to separate independent clauses in a sentence when the clauses contain closely related ideas. In this way, semicolons give readers a clue that the next idea is related. In contrast, use a period to introduce a new idea in the following sentence. This difference between semicolons and periods is illustrated below:

The slow food movement supports local production and consumption**;** it also emphasizes ethical eating.	(closely related information)
The slow food movement has gained support in recent years. The movement was originally seen as a reaction to the spread of fast food.	(new information)

Semicolons and Conjunctive Adverbs

You can also use semicolons in combination with conjunctive adverbs to separate closely related independent clauses:

The fair trade movement aims to improve the lives of small-scale farmers in developing countries**; however,** some farmers receive only minimal benefits.	(closely related information)
The fair trade movement aims to improve the lives of small-scale farmers in developing countries. **However,** some studies have shown that most consumers are more concerned about the price of products in their local supermarkets than about farmers' quality of life.	(new information)

Separating Items in a List

You have studied the use of commas to separate three or more items in a list. If one or more of the items contain a comma, you must use semicolons to separate them. Compare the examples below:

The fair trade movement needs to find strategies to address <u>expensive registration costs</u>**,** <u>excessive profits for intermediaries</u>**, and** <u>unstable product prices in world markets</u>.

The fair trade movement needs to find strategies to address <u>expensive registration costs, which disadvantage poor farmers</u>**;** <u>excessive profits for intermediaries</u>**; and** <u>unstable product prices in world markets, which fluctuate regularly</u>.

TASK 3

The following sentences are written without semicolons. Identify any places where commas or periods should be replaced with semicolons, and rewrite these parts of the sentences.

1. The fair trade movement has commendable aims. However, it has been argued that some intermediary buyers and sellers exploit the movement solely to make money for themselves.

   _____

   _____

2. Two of the most successful fair trade products are coffee and bananas. These two alone make up a large percentage of sales in richer countries.

   _____

   _____

3. Most shoppers can find fair trade coffee, bananas, and chocolate in local stores.

   _____

   _____

4. Most shoppers can find the following fair trade products in local stores: coffee, often imported from farms in Nicaragua, Kenya, and Colombia, bananas, primarily from Caribbean islands and Central America, and chocolate, made from cacao grown in countries such as Ivory Coast and Ghana.

   _____

   _____

TASK 4

Read the paragraph below. Replace periods with semicolons when you think ideas are closely related, and replace commas in lists with semicolons as needed.

Fair Trade

The fair trade movement dates back to the 1980s. Since its origin, thousands of small-scale farmers in developing countries have benefited from membership in fair trade programs. Today, the fair trade movement faces a number of challenges: fluctuating prices for products like coffee and bananas, which affect farmers' profits, mass-produced organic food, which competes in the ethical food market in developed countries, private and government intermediaries, who receive a percentage of every sale, and certification costs, which many small-scale farmers cannot afford. Certification costs should be the first problem to address. A reduction in these costs would allow more farmers to join and more profits to stay in local communities. Overall, fair trade has been a great success. However, the movement needs to become less *unfair* wherever possible.

TASK 5

Read the following paragraph, which is punctuated only with periods; it contains no commas or semicolons. Add commas and semicolons where necessary, and replace periods with semicolons when you think ideas are closely related.

Slow Food

The slow food movement is not just about eating slowly. It also relates to good and clean food. Agrillo Milano Roveglia and Scaffidi (2015) highlight two subjective factors in their definition of good food. The first is taste which relates to the subjective senses of the individual. The second is good knowledge of local culture environment and history of communities and their culinary practices. The role of promoting these values falls to local organizations called *convivia* established to educate people of all ages about "how food is produced and its production origins" (Page 2012 p. 3). Clearly the mission of slow food is to encourage lifestyles that promote good and clean food. However another important aspect is to eat in an ethically aware way.

Consumers have choices to make in their everyday interactions with food and the food industry. An example is the shopper who faces the decision to buy either a cheap mass-produced ready-made meal for microwaving or fresh local ingredients to cook the same meal from scratch. The slow food choice must be without doubt the latter.

My Bookshelf > My eLab > Exercises > Unit 5

SUMMARY   COMMAS AND SEMICOLONS

Function	Position	Examples
	Commas	
To set off extra information in an independent clause	Before the independent clause, following: a) a preposition phrase b) a conjunctive adverb c) a dependent clause d) a participle phrase	a) **Since the 1970s,** there has been a mandatory life sentence for murder in Canada. **Across the country,** the crime rate has fallen. b) **Moreover,** financially motivated crimes such as theft and burglary tend to rise during economic slowdowns. **However,** not all types of crimes have fallen continuously. c) **If unemployment rates fall,** violent crime rates also fall. **Although there is a link between crime and poverty,** other factors need to be considered. d) **Sensing a change in public opinion,** the government attempted to reinstate capital punishment in 1987. **Influenced by recent opinion polls,** the government attempted to reinstate capital punishment in 1987.
	Within the independent clause, to set off: a) a conjunctive adverb b) a non-defining relative clause c) a non-defining participle phrase d) a non-defining noun phrase	a) Financially motivated crimes such as theft and burglary, **moreover,** tend to rise during economic slowdowns. Not all types of crimes, **however,** have fallen continuously. b) The death penalty, **which is also known as *capital punishment*,** was abolished in Canada in 1976. After 1976, convicted murderers, **who previously might have received the death penalty,** would receive mandatory life sentences instead. c) In 1987, the government, **sensing a change in public opinion,** attempted to reinstate capital punishment. The death penalty, **also known as *capital punishment*,** was abolished in Canada in 1976. d) Youth unemployment, **a root cause of financially motivated crimes,** has gone up in the current economic slowdown.

Function	Position	Examples
To set off extra, non-defining information in an independent clause	After the independent clause, preceding: a) a conjunctive adverb b) a non-defining relative clause c) a non-defining participle phrase d) a non-defining noun phrase	a) Not all types of crimes have fallen continuously, **however**. b) Criminologists have studied the death penalty and deterrence, **which is its ability to prevent other crimes**. c) Criminologists often study the pros and cons of the death penalty, **also known as** *capital punishment*. d) The police are targeting burglary and car theft, **two of the most common financially motivated crimes**.
Coordination	Before the FANBOYS coordinators in compound sentences	Violent crime rates fell, **and** society became a lot safer. Violent crime rates fell, **but** those for online fraud rose. Mandatory life sentencing was introduced for murder, **so** the judiciary lost some of its independence.
	Between the items in lists of three or more things	Stricter environments mean inmates wear uniforms, books are limited, **and** lights are turned off at 10:30 p.m.
To separate adjectives before a noun	Between two or more adjectives of the same category	Prisoners are now expected to live in a **harsher, more punitive** environment.
Variations		
British English (omission of commas)	Before coordinators in compound sentences	Violent crime rates fell with the increased police presence **and** the city became safer in the months that followed.
	Before coordinators in lists of three or more things	Stricter environments mean inmates wear uniforms, books are limited **and** lights are turned off at 10:30 p.m.
Journalistic style (omission of commas)	After introductory preposition phrases	**Since the 1970s** there has been a mandatory life sentence for murder in Canada. **With the fall in crime** many people felt safer.
To avoid confusion (writers who usually omit commas)	After introductory phrases	**With the fall in crime,** prevention became more of a focus than punishment. (less confusing than "With the fall in crime prevention became …")
	Before coordinators that join two items	Inmates receive fewer comforts to make their stay in prison more tolerable and comfortable, **and** stricter punishments if they break any of the rules of prison life.
Personal preference	Writers may prefer not to use commas in some sentences if they feel it breaks the flow of the writing.	
Semicolons		
To separate independent clauses containing closely related information in a sentence	Between the independent clauses	The slow food movement supports local production and consumption; it also emphasizes ethical eating.
	After the first independent clause and before a conjunctive adverb	The fair trade movement aims to improve the lives of small-scale farmers in developing countries; **however,** some farmers receive only minimal benefits.
To separate three or more items in a list if one or more of the items contain a comma	Between the items in the list	The fair trade movement needs to find strategies to address expensive registration costs, which disadvantage poor farmers; excessive profits for intermediaries; **and** unstable product prices in world markets, which fluctuate regularly.

PARTICIPLE PHRASES

What Is a Participle Phrase?

Participle phrases (often called *participle clauses*) are similar to relative clauses. Both add information (defining or non-defining) about a thing or things in a related independent clause. Participle phrases follow the same rules of punctuation as those for relative clauses: commas are used to set off non-defining phrases, but not defining ones.

Participle phrases can be understood as reduced relative clauses. They usually express the same ideas as relative clauses, but in fewer words. In this way, participle phrases can give a sense of economy and add variety to your sentence structure.

The following examples illustrate how the relative clause (in italics) in sentence 1 can be reduced to a participle phrase (in bold) in sentence 2:

1. Fair trade products will become fairer when commodity producers receive a higher price, *which will bring benefits to local communities*.
2. Fair trade products will become fairer when commodity producers receive a higher price, **bringing benefits to local communities**.

In sentence 2, the present participle phrase *bringing benefits to local communities* expresses the idea conveyed by the relative clause in sentence 1, *which will bring benefits to local communities*.

Sentence 2 also illustrates an important feature of participle phrases, that is, the relationship between present and past participles does not correlate with present and past time. As can be seen in sentence 2, the present participle *bringing* refers to future time: "which will bring."

Present and Past Participle Phrases

As stated, the difference between present and past participle phrases does not relate to time. Present participle phrases are used as an alternative for clauses in the active voice, and past participle phrases, as an alternative for clauses in the passive voice.

The following sentences illustrate this difference.

Present Participle Phrases

1. Many registered fair trade coffee producers **living in Nicaragua** have invested in high registration costs in the hope of future benefits. (defining)
2. **Aiming for increased benefits for local communities**, Nicaraguan fair trade coffee producers campaigned for lower registration fees. (non-defining)

3. Fair trade producers will increase their market share in developed countries during the next 10 years, **leading to an increase in local development**. (non-defining)

Form: In the three phrases, the present participles are formed by adding *ing* to the verbs: *living*, *aiming*, and *leading*.

Concept: In the three example sentences, the participle phrases are used to convey the following meanings:

- Sentence 1: The participle phrase means "who live in."
- Sentence 2: The participle phrase means "because they were aiming for."
- Sentence 3: The participle phrase means "which will lead to" or "and it will lead to."

Time idea: Present participle phrases can be used with reference to past, present, or future time.

- Sentence 1 refers to present time: "who live in."
- Sentence 2 refers to past time: "because they were aiming for."
- Sentence 3 refers to future time: "which will lead to" or "and it will lead to."

Active voice: Present participle phrases are used in sentences in which the idea of the sentence would otherwise be expressed in an active-voice clause, as illustrated below.

Participle Phrase	Active-Voice Clause
Many registered fair trade coffee producers **living in Nicaragua** have invested in high registration costs in the hope of future benefits.	Many registered fair trade coffee producers who live in Nicaragua …
Aiming for increased benefits for local communities, Nicaraguan fair trade coffee producers campaigned for lower registration fees.	Because they were aiming for increased benefits for local communities, …
Fair trade producers will increase their market share in developed countries during the next 10 years, **leading to an increase in local development**.	… which will lead to an increase in local development.

Past Participle Phrases

1. The Fairtrade Labelling Organizations International (FLO), **set up in 1997**, coordinates registration and standards across the fair trade movement. (non-defining)
2. The FLO believes that money **received by local farmers** helps local communities to develop. (defining)
3. In the future, conscientious consumers will find an increasing variety of products **marked with fair trade logos**. (defining)

Form: In the three phrases, the first past participle is irregular (*set up*) while the second and third are regular, formed by adding *d* or *ed* to the verbs: *received*, *marked*.

Concept: In the three example sentences, the past participle phrases convey meaning in the same way as passive-voice sentences with regard to stated and unstated agents (the people or things doing the action).

- Sentence 1: The participle phrase *set up in 1997* has no stated agent as the agent is unknown or unimportant for the sentence.
- Sentence 2: The participle phrase *received by local farmers* emphasizes the stated agents (local farmers).
- Sentence 3: The participle phrase *marked with fair trade logos* has no stated agent as the agent is unimportant for the sentence.

Time idea: Past participle phrases can be used with reference to past, present, or future time.

- Sentence 1 refers to past time: "which was set up in."
- Sentence 2 refers to present time: "that is received by."
- Sentence 3 refers to future time: "that will be marked with."

Passive voice: Past participle phrases are used in sentences in which the idea of the sentence would otherwise be expressed in a passive-voice clause, as illustrated below.

Participle Phrase	Passive-Voice Clause
The Fairtrade Labelling Organizations International (FLO), **set up in 1997**, coordinates registration and standards across the fair trade movement.	The Fairtrade Labelling Organizations International (FLO), which was set up in 1997, . . .
The FLO believes that money **received by local farmers** helps local communities to develop.	The FLO believes that money that is received by local farmers . . .
In the future, conscientious consumers will find an increasing variety of products **marked with fair trade logos**.	. . . products that will be marked with fair trade logos.

TASK 1

<u>Underline</u> the participle phrase in each of the following sentences. Decide whether the participle phrase is replacing a clause in the active or passive voice and whether the participle phrase is present or past. Then state the time idea.

1. The slow food movement, originating in the 1980s, was a response to the spread of fast food restaurants in Italy.

    ☐ active voice ☐ passive voice ☐ present participle ☐ past participle

    Time idea: _____

2. Slow Food International, launched in 2001, brought greater worldwide attention to the movement.

    ☐ active voice ☐ passive voice ☐ present participle ☐ past participle

    Time idea: _____

3. Slow food promotes good, clean, and fair food for all, bringing together appreciation for the taste, culture, and local origins of food.

    ☐ active voice ☐ passive voice ☐ present participle ☐ past participle

    Time idea: _____

4. At slow food events, food produced by local farmers is showcased.

☐ active voice ☐ passive voice ☐ present participle ☐ past participle

Time idea: _____

5. In the future, it is hoped that slow food will spread globally, gaining a greater presence in large countries such as India and China.

☐ active voice ☐ passive voice ☐ present participle ☐ past participle

Time idea: _____

6. The benefits of ethical eating will be the focus of slow food events organized by future members of the movement.

☐ active voice ☐ passive voice ☐ present participle ☐ past participle

Time idea: _____

TASK 2

The following sentences contain relative clauses (in italics). First, rewrite each sentence, reducing the relative clause to a participle phrase. Then decide whether the participle phrase is replacing a clause in the active or passive voice and whether the participle phrase is present or past. Finally, state the time idea.

1. The fair trade movement, *which supports small-scale farmers and sustainability*, has a worldwide presence.

_____

_____

☐ active voice ☐ passive voice ☐ present participle ☐ past participle

Time idea: _____

2. Fair trade coffee and bananas, *which are grown primarily in Latin America and Africa*, are two of the best-selling products.

_____

_____

☐ active voice ☐ passive voice ☐ present participle ☐ past participle

Time idea: _____

3. A future goal of fair trade will be to tackle poverty more aggressively, *which will raise awareness of the need for a living wage for all farmers and their employees*.

_____

_____

☐ active voice ☐ passive voice ☐ present participle ☐ past participle

Time idea: _____

4. The move toward a living wage in fair trade will involve governments and international organizations as well as thousands of new farmers *who will be registered and certified as fair trade producers.*

_____

_____

_____

☐ active voice ☐ passive voice ☐ present participle ☐ past participle

Time idea: _____

5. In world markets *that are dominated by free trade*, the growth of fair trade alternatives may be slow.

_____

_____

_____

☐ active voice ☐ passive voice ☐ present participle ☐ past participle

Time idea: _____

6. Regulators need to address the problem of price reduction due to overproduction, *which occurs when farmers receive a premium for their product, overproduce, and thus create surpluses.*

_____

_____

_____

☐ active voice ☐ passive voice ☐ present participle ☐ past participle

Time idea: _____

My Bookshelf > My eLab > Exercises > Unit 6

TASK 3

Read the following excerpt from Suranovic, S. (2015). The meaning of fair trade. In L. T. Raynolds & E. A. Bennet (Eds.), Handbook of research on fair trade (pp. 45-60). Cheltenham, UK: Edward Elgar Publishing, and decide whether the words in bold form a participle phrase. Explain why or why not.

In the coffee industry, for example, from the early 1990s, four transnational companies—Nestlé, Phillip Morris, Sara Lee and Procter & Gamble—**accounted for more than 60 per cent of coffee sales in the major consuming markets**.

Participle phrase? ☐ Yes ☐ No

Why or why not?

_____

_____

PARTICIPLE PHRASES

Type	Example	Concept/Form
Defining	Many registered fair trade coffee producers **living in Nicaragua** have invested in high registration costs in the hope of future benefits.	• Essential information defining which coffee producers • No commas
Non-defining	The Fairtrade Labelling Organizations International (FLO), **set up in 1997**, coordinates registration and standards across the fair trade movement.	• Non-essential information about the FLO • Set off with commas
Present Participle Phrases		
Present participle phrases	Many registered fair trade coffee producers **living in Nicaragua** have invested in high registration costs in the hope of future benefits.	• Defining • Active-voice clause: "who live in Nicaragua" • Present time
	Aiming for increased benefits for local communities, Nicaraguan fair trade coffee producers campaigned for lower registration fees.	• Non-defining • Active-voice clause: "because they were aiming for . . ." • Past time
	Fair trade producers will increase their market share in developed countries during the next 10 years, **leading to an increase in local development.**	• Non-defining • Active-voice clause: "which will lead to / and it will lead to . . ." • Future time
Past Participle Phrases		
Past participle phrases	The Fairtrade Labelling Organizations International (FLO), **set up in 1997**, coordinates registration and standards across the fair trade movement.	• Non-defining • Passive-voice clause: "which was set up" • Past time
	The FLO believes that money **received by local farmers** helps local communities to develop.	• Defining • Passive-voice clause: "that is received by local farmers" • Present time
	In the future, conscientious consumers will find an increasing variety of products **marked with fair trade logos**.	• Defining • Passive-voice clause: "that will be marked with fair trade logos" • Future time

THE PASSIVE VOICE

The passive voice is commonly used in many forms of academic writing, particularly in forms that require an objective, scientific tone. Writing a sentence in the active or passive voice does not change the meaning. However, your choice to use one or the other can affect the tone that readers detect; it can also change the emphasis of information in the sentence in different ways.

Active and Passive Voice

The following examples show how to transform sentences in the active voice to the passive voice.

Active Voice

Active-voice sentences are formed with a subject followed by a corresponding verb, and sometimes an object:

1. Business leaders **require** sophisticated strategies when they work internationally.

subject	verb	object

2. Kamoche et al. (2015) **analyze** leadership strategies in Africa.

Passive Voice

To form a passive-voice sentence, place the object of an active-voice sentence in the subject position, use a form of the verb *to be* in the appropriate tense, and add a past participle:

1. Business leaders **require** sophisticated strategies when they work internationally. (active voice)

Sophisticated strategies **are required** in international work. (passive voice – no stated agent)

2. Kamoche et al. (2015) **analyze** leadership strategies in Africa. (active voice)

Leadership strategies in Africa **are analyzed** by Kamoche et al. (2015). (passive voice – stated agent: *by Kamoche et al. [2015]*)

The Passive Voice and Transitive Verbs

Passive-voice sentences are formed with transitive verbs, which are verbs that require an object. Intransitive verbs do not require an object. Some verbs can be used transitively or intransitively, depending on the context. In the active-voice examples below, the verbs are in bold and the objects, underlined.

Business leaders **face** <u>challenges</u> when they work internationally.	(transitive verb)
Leaders from Europe and Africa **talked** for three hours at the meeting.	(intransitive verb)
The European delegation **visited** <u>the site</u> three times.	(transitive or intransitive verb, used transitively)
The European delegation **visited** last year.	(transitive or intransitive verb, used intransitively)

TASK 1

Read the sentences below, and indicate whether the verbs are in the active or passive voice. If a verb is transitive and is in the active voice, rewrite the sentence in the passive voice. If a verb is in the passive voice, rewrite the sentence in the active voice. Key words to analyze and change are in bold.

1. **A recent study highlighted the need** to promote indigenous African knowledge in African transnational corporations.

   ☐ active voice   ☐ passive voice

   _____

   _____

2. In Section 3, **I will argue that** transcultural awareness is necessary in international business.

   ☐ active voice   ☐ passive voice

   _____

   _____

3. The role of women leaders in China, India, and Singapore **is discussed by** Peus, Braun, and Knipfer (2015).

   ☐ active voice   ☐ passive voice

   _____

   _____

4. **It has been documented that** Confucianism has greatly impacted leaders in the Chinese diaspora (Chai & Rhee, 2010).

   ☐ active voice   ☐ passive voice

   _____

   _____

5. It has been documented that **Confucianism has greatly impacted leaders** in the Chinese diaspora (Chai & Rhee, 2010).

   ☐ active voice   ☐ passive voice

   _____

   _____

6. **Scholars such as Kim and Moon (2015) and Peus, Braun, and Knipfer (2015) have addressed the relationship** between business leadership and local cultural knowledge.

   ☐ active voice   ☐ passive voice

   _____

   _____

The Passive Voice: Tone, Emphasis, and Agent

Use of the passive voice as opposed to the active voice does not change meaning. However, it can affect the tone of the sentence and the emphasis of information, as illustrated below.

Active Voice

1. Business leaders require sophisticated strategies when they work internationally.
2. Kim and Moon (2015) analyze leadership strategies in Asia.

Tone: Sentences 1 and 2 have an academic tone due to the vocabulary (*require, analyze*). The fact that they are in the active voice rather than the passive voice has little effect on their tone.

Emphasis: In sentence 1, the use of the active voice has little effect on which part of the sentence is emphasized. In sentence 2, *Kim and Moon (2015) analyze* is a citation phrase: *Kim and Moon* is the subject of the reporting verb *analyze*. In citation phrases, use of the active voice, with the author(s) as the subject of a reporting verb, can emphasize the author more than the information cited.

Passive Voice

1. Sophisticated strategies are required in international work. (passive voice with no stated agent)
2. Leadership strategies in Asia are analyzed by Kim and Moon (2015). (passive voice – stated agent: *by Kim and Moon [2015]*)

Tone: Sentences 1 and 2 have an academic tone due to the vocabulary (*require, analyze*) and the use of the passive voice. The passive voice adds an extra tone of scientific objectivity.

Emphasis: In sentence 1, there is no stated agent: the writer does not indicate who requires the sophisticated strategies. This type of agentless passive-voice sentence is used here because the agent is unknown or unimportant and because the information in the sentence is a generally accepted fact. In this case, the stated strategies are more important than knowing who requires them. In sentence 2, the agent is stated: *Kim and Moon (2015)*. In this type of passive-voice sentence, the agent is emphasized.

TASK 2

Rewrite the following active-voice sentences as passive-voice sentences, following the prompts in parentheses. Explain your decisions about whether or not to state the agents.

1. In Section 2, I argue that traditional forms of knowledge in Africa and Asia should be seen as resources for business leaders.

   (Write a passive-voice sentence beginning with *it will* to create a less personal tone. Decide whether to add emphasis by stating the agent.)

   _____

   _____

   _____

   _____

   _____

2. Scholars such as Kim and Moon (2015) and Peus, Braun, and Knipfer (2015) have suggested that business leadership should be more closely tied to local cultural knowledge.

   (Write a passive-voice sentence beginning with *it has*. Decide whether to state the agent.)

   _____

   _____

   _____

   _____

   _____

Agentless Passives

Passive-voice sentences with no stated agent are also called *agentless passives*. Agentless passives are used when the agent is unknown or considered to be unimportant. In cases of factual statements based on common knowledge, agentless passives pose few problems. However, in academic writing, agentless passives are problematic when the writer claims to represent the ideas of experts without stating explicitly who these experts are.

1. Local cultural knowledge was passed on orally before writing systems emerged.

2. It has been argued that intercultural awareness is as important as traditional leadership skills in business.

3. It has been argued that business leaders should pay more attention to local knowledge and culture.

In sentence 1, the agent is unknown and unimportant for the focus of the sentence. The sentence is not problematic because it states a generally recognized fact.

Sentence 2 has no stated agent. This example is problematic because the writer should state clearly who has put forward this argument. Similarly, sentence 3 is problematic because the writer should state who has argued this point about business leaders.

Passive-Voice Sentences with *to Get*

It is also possible to write passive-voice sentences using *to get* as the auxiliary verb in place of *to be*. Using *get* with the passive voice is more common in informal English than in formal academic style. It can also cause a change in meaning, suggesting the information conveyed is surprising or unpleasant.

1. My thesis proposal **was** rejected.
2. My thesis proposal **got** rejected.

In sentence 2, the writer has used *got* instead of *was* as the auxiliary verb in the passive-voice sentence, adding a sense of unexpectedness or unpleasantness to it. As such, the reader may interpret the sentence to mean that the writer was expecting the proposal to be accepted and is surprised or annoyed.

TASK 3

Read the following active- and passive-voice sentences, and answer the questions that follow.

1. My laptop was stolen yesterday afternoon. I left it in the room during the lunch break.

   Does the speaker seem surprised or annoyed?

   _____

2. I just found out that I got accepted for the scholarship!

   Does it seem like the speaker was expecting to be accepted?

   _____

3. The view that the MMR vaccine causes autism has been discredited.

   Why might an instructor add a margin note that asks, "By whom?"

   _____

4. The view that the MMR vaccine causes autism has been discredited by leading scientists.

   Why might an instructor add a margin note that asks, "Which ones?"

   _____

   _____

5. Leadership strategies in Asia are analyzed by Kim and Moon (2015).

   Does this sentence emphasize the agent?

   _____

My Bookshelf > My eLab > Exercises > Unit 7

Voice	Examples	Form/Concept
Active voice	Business leaders **require** sophisticated strategies when they work internationally. Kamoche et al. (2015) **analyze** leadership strategies in Africa.	Form: subject + **verb** + object
Passive voice	a) Sophisticated strategies **are required** in international work. (no stated agent) b) Leadership strategies in Africa **are analyzed** by Kamoche et al. (2015). (stated agent)	• Active-voice object moves to subject position in the passive voice. • Form: *to be* + past participle • Verb must be transitive. • a) No stated agent b) Stated agent: *by Kamoche et al. (2015)*
Stating the Agent		
Passive voice, no stated agent	a) Sophisticated strategies are required in international work. b) Local cultural knowledge was passed on orally before writing systems emerged. c) It has been argued that business leaders should pay more attention to local knowledge and culture.	a) Agent is unimportant. b) Agent is unknown and unimportant for the sentence. c) Unstated agent is problematic: writer needs to state who the idea or argument belongs to.
Passive voice, stated agent	Leadership strategies in Asia are analyzed **by Kim and Moon (2015)**.	The agent is important for the sentence and is given emphasis.
Tone		
Active voice	In Section 3, I will argue that transcultural awareness is necessary in international business.	Personal, subjective style
Passive voice	In Section 3, it will be argued that transcultural awareness is necessary in international business.	Less personal, more objective style
Passive Voice with *to Get*		
Passive voice with *to be*	My thesis proposal **was** rejected.	Neutral
Passive voice with *to get*	My thesis proposal **got** rejected.	Sense of unexpectedness or unpleasantness

PUNCTUATION: COLONS AND APOSTROPHES

The rules for colons and apostrophes are not always agreed on in academic writing, nor are they always followed consistently. You will likely notice that writers use colons and apostrophes differently. This may be because they have followed a publisher's style guidelines, which are usually based on slightly different rules set out by organizations such as the APA and MLA. It may also be because they do not know how to use these punctuation marks correctly!

The following are the most common rules for colons and apostrophes.

COLONS · THREE USES OF COLONS

Colons are used to introduce examples and lists at the end of an independent clause, and to introduce direct quotations, also at the end of an independent clause. In addition, they are commonly used to separate main titles from subtitles when referring to written works.

Introducing Examples and Lists

Use a colon to introduce a list or examples after an independent clause:

> Two key factors affect business in Africa: globalization and dominant Western business practices.

Do not use a colon to introduce a list or examples that are incorporated grammatically into the sentence:

> Two key factors affecting business in Africa **are** globalization and dominant Western business practices.

Use a colon to create an economical style in a list containing long items. Compare the following paragraphs:

> In the above sections, I analyzed several factors related to business between Asia, Africa, and the West. First, I looked at strategies that promote intercultural understanding between regions. Second, I focused on the effects of globalization and dominant Western business practices in African and Asian countries. Finally, I considered the potential of crossvergence as opposed to convergence and divergence in international leadership.

> In the above sections, I analyzed the following factors related to business between Asia, Africa, and the West: strategies that promote intercultural understanding between regions, the effects of globalization and dominant Western business practices in African and Asian countries, and the potential of crossvergence as opposed to convergence and divergence in international leadership.

The items in the examples are separated by commas. If one of the items contained a comma, semicolons would be used to separate the items (see Unit 5, p. 34).

In the second paragraph, the insertion of a colon has taken away the need to use introductory linking words such as *first* and *second* as well as verb phrases such as *I looked at* and *I focused on*. Instead, with the colon, the list of noun phrases is sufficient.

Introducing Direct Quotations

Use a colon to introduce direct quotations at the end of an independent clause:

> Leadership assessments must be conducted as follows: "in a structured manner, primarily based on behavioral criteria" (Peus et al., 2012, p. 106).

Do not use a colon to introduce a direct quotation that is incorporated grammatically into the sentence:

> Leadership assessments should "be conducted in a structured manner, primarily based on behavioral criteria" (Peus et al., 2012, p. 106).

Separating a Main Title and a Subtitle

In titles of books, articles, and essays, it is common to use a colon to separate the main title (which indicates the general topic) and the subtitle (which shows the specific focus).

> Business Leadership in Africa: Rising to the Challenge

> Leadership Strategies in Chinese Corporations: Looking West or East?

TASK 1

Indicate whether the following sentences are correct or incorrect. If the sentence is incorrect, rewrite it.

1. Three trends in international business leadership have been analyzed: convergence, divergence, and crossvergence.

   ☐ correct   ☐ incorrect

   _____

   _____

2. The three trends studied for international business leadership are: convergence, divergence, and crossvergence.

   ☐ correct   ☐ incorrect

   _____

   _____

3. According to a famous entrepreneur, "business is 10% theory and 90% common sense."

   ☐ correct   ☐ incorrect

   _____

   _____

4. A famous entrepreneur once stated that: "business is 10% theory and 90% common sense."

☐ correct ☐ incorrect

_____

_____

TASK 2

Insert a colon in the paragraph below and rewrite it in a more economical style.

Entrepreneurial Assets

Establishing a successful new business is not a simple task. Anyone trying to succeed needs the following. First, it is essential to find a niche in the market and a product to sell in that space. Second, the entrepreneur needs to develop a sound marketing plan, with a clear focus on product, price, and placement. Third, he or she needs to guarantee quality and consistency in the production process. Finally, any entrepreneur starting a new project needs to be able to learn from mistakes.

_____

_____

_____

_____

_____

APOSTROPHES | # TWO USES OF APOSTROPHES

Apostrophes are used mainly for possessives (showing that something belongs to something or someone) and contractions (short forms such as *doesn't* instead of *does not*). For possessives, the position of the apostrophe depends on whether the noun it is added to is singular or plural.

Possessives

To form the possessive of a singular noun, add an apostrophe and an *s*:

Intercultural awareness can help **a business leader's decision-making** in international contexts.

For a singular noun ending in *s*, add an apostrophe and an *s*. Note, however, that some writers add only an apostrophe in such cases.

A clear marketing plan can promote **a business's growth** in its initial years.

A clear marketing plan can promote **a business' growth** in its initial years.

For a plural noun ending in *s*, add an apostrophe:

Intercultural awareness has an inevitable effect on **business leaders' beliefs**, values, and actions.

For a plural noun not ending in *s*, add an apostrophe and an *s*:

> Many factors affect **women's chances** for advancement to leadership positions in international corporations.

For two or more individual possessives, add an apostrophe to each:

> **Guo's** (2015) and **Li's** (2016) **analyses** of crossvergence in Asian contexts provide useful recommendations for international business leaders.

Note that the example above refers to two separate studies, so they qualify as individual possessives.

For joint possessives, add only one apostrophe to the final person or thing:

> **Kim and Moon's** (2015) **analysis** of Corporate Social Responsibility (CSR) focuses on practices in several Asian countries.

Note that the example above refers to one co-authored study, so it qualifies as a joint possessive.

For a place name that ends with a plural noun ending in *s*, add an apostrophe:

> **The Unites States' historical position** in support of free trade agreements may change in the next 20 years.

For an indefinite pronoun (e.g., *anyone*, *someone*), add an apostrophe and an *s*:

> **Someone's bag** was left at the meeting.

For a name not ending in *s*, add an apostrophe and an *s*:

> **Lee's CSR plan** was accepted by the board.

For a name ending in *s*, add an apostrophe and an *s*. Note, however, that some writers add only an apostrophe in such cases.

> **Carlos's CSR plan** was accepted by the board.
> **Carlos' CSR plan** was accepted by the board.

Awkward Possessive Apostrophes

Avoid using apostrophes that make words or phrases awkward to read or say.

For example, avoid sentences with too many possessives grouped together:

> **Ms. Lee's company's representative's proposal** was accepted.

Rephrase such sentences to make them more readable:

> The proposal put forward by the representative of **Ms. Lee's company** was accepted.

With names ending in an *s* pronounced *eez*, the pronunciation may become awkward by adding an extra *s*, so many writers use only the apostrophe.

> **Mr. Davies' CSR plan** was accepted by the board.

Note that it is easier to pronounce *Mr. Davies'* than *Mr. Davies's*.

Contractions

Contractions are shortened words with a letter or letters omitted. They are often avoided in academic writing due to the perception that they can make the tone informal. Nonetheless, some writers use them; the choice to do so depends on the genre of writing, the reader(s), or the writer's personal preference.

Examples of Common Contractions

Negative Verbs	Subjects + Auxiliary Verbs
isn't (is not)	**I'm** (I am)
aren't (are not)	**I've** (I have)
hasn't (has not)	**you're** (you are)
haven't (have not)	**you've** (you have)
don't (do not)	**she's** (she is)
won't (will not)	**he'll** (he will)
wouldn't (would not)	**they're** (they are)
shouldn't (should not)	**they'd** (they would)

Numbers may also be contracted, specifically, in abbreviated forms of years, used in less formal English:

During the **'90s** (During the 1990s)

Contraction Errors

The following are common errors to avoid when you use apostrophes in contractions.

***Its* and *it's*:** When *its* is used as a possessive, do not add an apostrophe. When *it's* is used as a contraction of *it is* or *it has*, add an apostrophe.

✓ The company is rebranding **its** logo.

✗ The company is rebranding **it's** logo.

✓ **It's** time we left.

✗ **Its** time we left.

***Whose* and *who's*:** Avoid confusing *whose* (a possessive relative pronoun) and *who's* (a contraction of *who is*).

✓ **Whose** idea are you using?

✗ **Who's** idea are you using?

✓ **Who's** been helping you with the proposal?

✗ **Whose** been helping you with the proposal?

Other possessive pronouns that never contain an apostrophe are *ours*, *yours*, *his*, *hers*, and *theirs*.

✓ The idea was **ours**.

✗ The idea was **our's**.

***Should've* and *should of*:** The contracted form of *should have* is *should've*. Some writers make the mistake of writing *should of* due to the similar pronunciation.

✓ We **should've** considered their proposal.

✗ We **should of** considered their proposal.

***Your* and *you're*:** *Your* is a possessive adjective. *You're* is the contraction of *you are*.

✓ It was **your** idea.

✗ It was **you're** idea.

✓ **You're** meeting us this afternoon.

✗ **Your** meeting us this afternoon.

Years in reference to periods, such as *the 1980s*: Many writers incorrectly add an apostrophe after years when referring to the decade.

✓ During the **1980s**, there was a global economic recession.

✗ During the **1980's**, there was a global economic recession.

TASK 3

Indicate whether the following sentences are correct or incorrect. If the sentence is incorrect, rewrite it.

1. Dealing with a glass ceiling can be a woman business leaders main hindrance to progress.

   ☐ correct   ☐ incorrect

   _____

   _____

2. The class's requests were dealt with by the course director.

   ☐ correct   ☐ incorrect

   _____

3. The classes' requests were dealt with by the course director.

   ☐ correct   ☐ incorrect

   _____

4. The marketing class analyzed the advertising of childrens products.

   ☐ correct   ☐ incorrect

   _____

   _____

5. The CEOs and managers roles in the company were very different.

   ☐ correct   ☐ incorrect

   _____

   _____

6. The United Arab Emirates oil reserves total almost 100 billion barrels.

   ☐ correct   ☐ incorrect

   _____

   _____

7. Is this anyones phone?

☐ correct   ☐ incorrect

_____

8. Linda's office is the second on the left.

☐ correct   ☐ incorrect

_____

9. Charles office is next to Lindas'.

☐ correct   ☐ incorrect

_____

10. Dont be late for the meeting; your going to get an answer to your request for more staff.

☐ correct   ☐ incorrect

_____

_____

11. Its time for the management to review it's procedures.

☐ correct   ☐ incorrect

_____

TASK 4

The following paragraph contains no colons or apostrophes. Add them as required.

Richard Branson: Entrepreneur and Adventurer

Richard Branson, one of the worlds most famous entrepreneurs, set up Virgin Records in the early 70s in London, England. In the next 20 years, a radio station, an airline, and a phone company were added to the Virgin brand Virgin Radio, Virgin Atlantic Airways, and Virgin Mobile. By the middle of the 2000s, Bransons new company for space tourism, Virgin Galactic, was up and running. Branson has also caught peoples attention with his attempts at breaking world records, including an attempt to cross the Atlantic in a hot-air balloon. In 1987, Branson and a Swede, Per Lindstrand, set off to make the first transatlantic balloon flight. Branson and Lindstrands attempt went famously wrong when they had to jump into the ocean and be rescued. Branson was undeterred. His attitude to success and failure can be best summed up by the following quotation "Dont be embarrassed by your failures. Learn from them and start again."

My Bookshelf > My eLab >
Exercises > Unit 8

Function	Context	Examples
Colons		
To introduce a list or examples	After an independent clause *Do not use a colon when the list or examples are incorporated grammatically in the sentence.	Two key factors affect business in Africa**:** globalization and dominant Western business practices. *Two key factors affecting business in Africa are globalization and dominant Western business practices.
	After an independent clause, to create an economical style	**Less economical style:** In the above sections, I analyzed several factors related to business between Asia, Africa, and the West. First, I looked at strategies that . . . . Second, I focused on the effects of . . . . Finally, I considered the potential of crossvergence as opposed to . . . **More economical style:** In the above sections, I analyzed several factors related to business between Asia, Africa, and the West**:** strategies that . . ., the effects of . . ., and the potential of crossvergence as opposed to . . .
To introduce direct quotations	After an independent clause *Do not use a colon when the direct quotation is incorporated grammatically in the sentence.	Leadership assessments must be conducted as follows**:** "in a structured manner, primarily based on behavioral criteria" (Peus et al., 2012, p. 106). *Leadership assessments should "be conducted in a structured manner, primarily based on behavioral criteria" (Peus et al., 2012, p. 106).
To separate a main title and a subtitle	In titles of books, articles, and essays	Business Leadership in Africa**:** Rising to the Challenge Leadership Strategies in Chinese Corporations**:** Looking West or East?
Apostrophes		
To indicate possession	Singular nouns not ending in *s* **Rule:** Add *'s*.	Intercultural awareness can help **a business leader's decision-making** in international contexts.
	Singular nouns ending in *s* **Rule:** Add *'s* or only the apostrophe.	A clear marketing plan can promote **a business's/business' growth** in its initial years.
	Plural nouns ending in *s* **Rule:** Add only the apostrophe.	Intercultural awareness has an inevitable effect on **business leaders' beliefs**, values, and actions.
	Plural nouns not ending in *s* **Rule:** Add *'s*.	Many factors affect **women's chances** for advancement to leadership positions in international corporations.
	Two or more individual possessives **Rule:** Add *'s* to each possessive noun.	**Guo's** (2015) and **Li's** (2016) **analyses** of crossvergence in Asian contexts provide useful recommendations for international business leaders.
	Joint possessives **Rule:** Add *'s* only to the last possessive noun.	**Kim and Moon's** (2015) **analysis** of Corporate Social Responsibility (CSR) focuses on practices in several Asian countries.
	Place names ending with a plural noun that ends in *s* **Rule:** Add only the apostrophe.	**The Unites States' historical position** in support of free trade agreements may change in the next 20 years.
	Indefinite pronouns **Rule:** Add *'s*.	**Someone's bag** was left at the meeting.

Function	Context	Examples	
To indicate possession	Names not ending in *s* **Rule:** Add *'s*.	**Lee's CSR plan** was accepted by the board.	
	Names ending in *s* **Rule:** Add *'s* or only the apostrophe.	**Carlos's/Carlos' CSR plan** was accepted by the board.	
Contractions	Negative verbs	**isn't** (is not) **aren't** (are not) **hasn't** (has not) **haven't** (have not)	**don't** (do not) **won't** (will not) **wouldn't** (would not) **shouldn't** (should not)
	Subject + auxiliary verbs	**I'm** (I am) **I've** (I have) **you're** (you are) **you've** (you have)	**she's** (she is) **he'll** (he will) **they're** (they are) **they'd** (they would)
	Abbreviated forms of years (less formal)	During the **'90s** (During the 1990s)	
Avoiding contraction errors	*its* versus *it's*	The company is rebranding **its** logo. **It's** time we left.	
	whose versus *who's*	**Whose** idea are you using? **Who's** been helping you with the proposal?	
	Other possessive pronouns: *ours, yours, his, hers, theirs* **Rule:** No apostrophe.	The idea was **ours**.	
	should've versus *should of*	We **should've** considered their proposal.	
	your versus *you're*	It was **your** idea. **You're** meeting us this afternoon.	
	Years referring to a decade **Rule:** No apostrophe.	During the **1980s**, there was a global economic recession.	

UNIT 9

SENTENCE FRAGMENTS, COMMA SPLICES, AND RUN-ON SENTENCES

Sentence Fragments

A sentence fragment is an incomplete sentence because it lacks at least one required component of an independent clause. The following sections describe the three most common types of sentence fragment.

Dependent Clause Written as a Complete Sentence

> Even though the aims of the fair trade movement are laudable.

The sentence begins with the subordinator *even though*, which makes the clause dependent. In informal conversation or digital communication, this type of sentence fragment is commonly used as a sentence. However, in academic writing, it needs to be corrected in one of the following two ways.

Remove the subordinator:

> ~~Even though~~ The aims of the fair trade movement are laudable.

OR

Connect the dependent clause to an independent clause, forming a complex sentence:

> Even though the aims of the fair trade movement are laudable, **it still needs to reform**.

It may be helpful to refer to Appendix 1, Linking Words (page 101), and Unit 3, Three Types of Sentence (page 18) as you study this Unit, to review the following: subordinators, coordinators, and conjunctive adverbs; compound and complex sentences.

Sentence without a Verb

> The slow food movement a challenge to fast-food culture.

This sentence fragment would work well as a headline of a news article if a colon was added:

> The slow food movement: a challenge to fast-food culture

However, to become a complete sentence, the fragment needs a verb:

> The slow food movement **represents** a challenge to fast-food culture.

Sentence without a Subject

> Gave the presentation on rehabilitation last night!

This type of sentence fragment is common in informal digital communication, for example, on social networking sites. However, in academic writing, a sentence needs a subject:

> **She** gave the presentation on rehabilitation last night.

Note also the removal of the exclamation mark in formal academic writing.

TASK 1

Correct the five sentence fragments below so that they become complete sentences.

1. Despite local farmers receiving a higher price for fair trade products.

_____

_____

2. Fast-food culture spreading worldwide.

_____

_____

3. Excessive fast-food consumption health problems in later life.

_____

_____

4. Discussed trading issues between southern Africa and the EU yesterday!

_____

_____

5. Because intermediaries make considerable profits in the fair trade chain.

_____

_____

Comma Splices

Comma splices are the result of the incorrect separation of two independent clauses with a comma instead of a semicolon or period.

Two Independent Clauses Separated by a Comma

Excessive fast-food consumption can lead to weight gain, it can also cause health problems in later life.

To correct the comma splice, replace the comma with a period or semicolon. In this case, the semicolon is preferable because the two clauses are closely related.

Excessive fast-food consumption can lead to weight gain**;** it can also cause health problems in later life.

Excessive fast-food consumption can lead to weight gain**. It** can also cause health problems in later life.

Another way to correct the comma splice is to form a compound sentence, using *and* or *not only*:

Excessive fast-food consumption can lead to weight gain, **and** it can cause health problems in later life.

Not only can excessive fast-food consumption lead to weight gain, it can also cause health problems in later life.

> Learn more about how to invert sentence structures for emphasis with negative adverbial phrases such as *Not only* in Unit 14 Inversion for Emphasis.

Two Independent Clauses Separated by a Conjunctive Adverb with a Comma

> Local farmers receive a higher price for fair trade products, however, many still live in poverty.

To correct the comma splice, replace the comma at the end of the first independent clause with a semicolon or period. Again, the semicolon is preferable in this case because the two clauses are closely related.

> Local farmers receive a higher price for fair trade products**;** however, many still live in poverty.

> Local farmers receive a higher price for fair trade products**.** **However**, many still live in poverty.

You can also correct the comma splice by rewriting the sentence with a coordinator such as *but* or *yet* to form a compound sentence:

> Local farmers receive a higher price for fair trade products, **but/yet** many still live in poverty.

A third way to correct the comma splice is to rewrite the sentence with a subordinator such as *although* or *while* to form a complex sentence:

> **Although/While** local farmers receive a higher price for fair trade products, many still live in poverty.

Comma Splices and Genre

In some non-academic genres of writing, for example, literary writing and journalism, comma splices are used and deemed acceptable. Comma splices are also common in informal communication.

TASK 2

Correct the four comma splices below, using at least two of the methods described above. Use a semicolon rather than a period to join independent clauses with closely related ideas.

1. The Mediterranean diet has been shown to reduce the incidence of cardiovascular disease, it may also prevent certain types of cancer.

   _____

   _____

   _____

   _____

2. Local farmers receive a higher price for fair trade products, therefore, consumers have to pay a premium at the supermarket.

   _____

   _____

   _____

   _____

3. Fast-food culture has grown worldwide due to lifestyle changes and marketing, nonetheless, traditional food is still preferred in many countries around the globe.

_____

_____

_____

_____

4. Today's international business leaders need to understand many different cultures, this is easier if they speak several languages.

_____

_____

_____

_____

Run-On Sentences

A run-on sentence is a sentence in which two or more independent clauses are joined without punctuation. Run-on sentences should be corrected in the same ways as the comma splices above.

> Excessive fast-food consumption can lead to weight gain it can also cause health problems in later life.

In the example above, there is no punctuation between the first independent clause, ending with *weight gain*, and the second one, beginning with *it*.

> The Mediterranean diet has been shown to reduce the incidence of cardiovascular disease it may also prevent certain types of cancer.

Here there is no punctuation between the first independent clause, ending with *cardiovascular disease*, and the second one, beginning with *it*.

Correct run-on sentences by adding a semicolon or period, or by modifying the sentence structure, as shown above in the section on comma splices.

TASK 3

Correct the following run-on sentences by applying at least two of the methods you have studied in this unit.

1. Fast-food consumption is on the rise worldwide young people in many countries are now eating more fast food and less local food.

_____

_____

_____

_____

2. The slow food movement promotes healthy and ethical eating it emerged as a reaction to the spread of fast-food culture.

_____

_____

_____

_____

TASK 4

The paragraph below contains sentence fragments, comma splices, and run-on sentences. Rewrite the paragraph, correcting the errors by applying the methods you have studied in this unit.

The Mediterranean Diet

The Mediterranean diet gets its name, unsurprisingly, from the food eaten in countries surrounding the Mediterranean Sea. Even though many of these foods are also eaten elsewhere in the world. The diet is characterized by high consumption of extra virgin olive oil, whole grains, green vegetables, and fresh fruit, dairy products and fish tend to be consumed moderately. Red meat and saturated fat are consumed much less. As are processed foods. Another important feature of the Mediterranean diet is a social dimension, meals are often eaten together as a family unit. Not in front of the TV or during a 10-minute lunch break. A number of studies have found that the Mediterranean diet can prevent heart disease, cancer, and diabetes in later life it has also been found to increase longevity.

_____

_____

_____

_____

_____

_____

_____

_____

_____

My Bookshelf > My eLab >
Exercises > Unit 9

SENTENCE FRAGMENTS, COMMA SPLICES, AND RUN-ON SENTENCES

Problem	Examples	Correction Methods
Sentence Fragments		
Dependent clause written as a complete sentence	Even though the aims of the fair trade movement are laudable.	a) Remove the subordinator: The aims of the fair trade movement are laudable. b) Form a complex sentence: Even though the aims of the fair trade movement are laudable, **it still needs to reform**.
Sentence without a verb	The slow food movement a challenge to fast-food culture.	Add a verb: The slow food movement **represents** a challenge to fast-food culture.
Sentence without a subject	Gave the presentation on rehabilitation last night!	Add a subject: **She** gave the presentation on rehabilitation last night.
Comma Splices		
Two independent clauses separated by a comma	Excessive fast-food consumption can lead to weight gain, it can also cause health problems in later life.	a) Replace the comma with a semicolon or period: Excessive fast-food consumption can lead to weight gain**;** it can also cause health problems in later life. (preferable because the ideas are closely related) Excessive fast-food consumption can lead to weight gain**.** **It** can also cause health problems in later life. b) Form a compound sentence with *and* or use *not only*: Excessive fast-food consumption can lead to weight gain, **and** it can cause health problems in later life. **Not only** can excessive fast-food consumption lead to weight gain, it can also cause health problems in later life.
Two independent clauses separated by a conjunctive adverb with a comma	Local farmers receive a higher price for fair trade products, however, many still live in poverty.	a) Replace the first comma with a semicolon or period: Local farmers receive a higher price for fair trade products**;** however, many still live in poverty. Local farmers receive a higher price for fair trade products**.** **However**, many still live in poverty. b) Form a compound sentence, adding a coordinator: Local farmers receive a higher price for fair trade products, **but/yet** many still live in poverty. c) Form a complex sentence, adding a subordinator: **Although/While** local farmers receive a higher price for fair trade products, many still live in poverty.
Run-On Sentences		
No punctuation joining independent clauses	a) Excessive fast-food consumption can lead to weight gain it can also cause health problems in later life. b) The Mediterranean diet has been shown to reduce the incidence of cardiovascular disease it may also prevent certain types of cancer.	Replace the comma with a semicolon or period, or modify the sentence structure (as for comma splices): a) Excessive fast-food consumption can lead to weight gain**;** it can also cause health problems in later life. b) **Not only** has the Mediterranean diet been shown to reduce the incidence of cardiovascular disease, it may also prevent certain types of cancer.

UNIT 10

SUBJECT-VERB AGREEMENT

Subject-verb agreement means that subjects and their corresponding verbs should agree. In other words, if the subject is singular, the verb should be in a singular form; if the subject is plural, the verb should be in a plural form. While this may seem simple, there are some rules to learn to ensure that subjects and verbs agree consistently and accurately in your writing. The examples below illustrate some common rules for subject-verb agreement. The subjects are underlined and the corresponding verbs, in bold.

Basic Rules

For main verbs in the present tense, except irregular verbs such as *to be*, the third-person singular form requires an *s*. The other forms do not.

> 3D printing **involves** using plastic or metal powders to create copies of objects.

> 3D printers **form** thousands of horizontal layers to create objects.

For tenses with auxiliary verbs—for example, perfect, continuous, and future tenses—only the auxiliary verb agrees with the subject. Modal auxiliary verbs, however, do not change form in the third-person singular.

> In the last 10 years, air pollution **has damaged** more local environments.

> Air pollutants **are having** a particularly negative effect on urban environments.

> Pollutant levels in the EU **will** most likely **fall** further in the next decade.

> Air pollution **may rise** further if no action is taken.

Compound Subjects

A compound subject is made up of two or more nouns or pronouns, for example, A and B, X or Y.

Compound Subjects with *And*

If the subject of the sentence comprises two or more nouns or pronouns plus *and*, use the plural form of the verb:

> Ammonia and nitrogen dioxide **are** two major air pollutants.

> Pollution, pesticides, and fast food **have been linked** to ill health in children.

In some cases, however, two nouns joined by *and* represent a single idea and require a singular verb:

> Research and development into reducing air pollution **is** ongoing.

Compound Subjects with *Or* and *Nor*

If the subject of the sentence comprises two or more singular nouns or pronouns joined by *or* or *nor*, use the singular form of the verb:

> Fast food or lack of a balanced diet often **leads** to ill health in children.

> Neither fast food nor unhealthy eating fully **explains** why children become ill.

If the compound subject is made up of a combination of singular and plural nouns joined by *or* or *nor*, the verb should agree with the nearest noun or pronoun in the subject:

> Fast food or unhealthy eating habits often **lead** to ill health in children.

Compound Subjects with *As Well As* and *Along With*

If the compound subject is formed by two or more nouns or pronouns joined by *as well as* or *along with*, the corresponding verb should agree with the first noun in the subject. Compare the following sentences:

> Fast food, unhealthy eating, and lack of exercise **are** bad for children's health.

> Fast food, along with unhealthy eating and lack of exercise, **is** bad for children's health.

Indefinite Pronouns

Indefinite pronouns are pronouns that do not refer to a specific person, thing, or place, for example, *everyone*, *somebody*, *each*, and *neither*. Sentences with indefinite pronouns acting as subjects follow specific rules of subject-verb agreement.

Use a Singular Verb

When they form the subject of a sentence, the following indefinite pronouns require a singular verb: *another*, *anybody*, *anyone*, *anything*, *each* (one), *either*, *everybody*, *everyone*, *everything*, *neither*, *nobody*, *no one*, *nothing*, *one*, *other*, *somebody*, *someone*, and *something*.

> In my opinion, nothing **is** impossible with 3D printing.

> Something **isn't working** properly in the machine.

Use a Plural Verb

Use the plural form of the verb in sentences with the following indefinite pronouns as subjects: *both*, *few*, *many*, *others*, and *several*.

> A variety of objects today are made by 3D printing; many **are** prototypes.

> The workshop is now equipped with a 3D printer as well as a multifunction printer; both **require** regular maintenance.

Use a Singular or a Plural Verb

Some indefinite pronouns, for example, *all*, *none*, and *some*, may be followed by a singular or plural verb, depending on the context (whether they refer to a singular or plural noun).

> All of the objects on display **were made** with a 3D printer.

> All of the machinery **is** less than a year old.

Collective Nouns

Collective nouns are used to refer to groups of things or people. In most cases, they require singular verbs (although plural verbs may be used in less formal contexts). Some examples of collective nouns are *class*, *crowd*, *family*, *government*, *group*, *organization*, *population*, and *team*.

> The Environmental Sciences class **is going** on a field trip next week.
>
> The Environmental Sciences class **are collecting** samples. (informal)
>
> The government **has increased** funding for non-polluting fuel systems.

Plural verbs can also be used with collective nouns, when the members of the group are acting as individuals rather than together.

> The Environmental Sciences class **are doing** their individual projects.

TASK 1

Some of the following sentences have incorrect, or informal, subject-verb agreement. Identify the incorrect sentences and rewrite them.

1. In the last 10 years, air pollution phenomena has increased.

   ☐ correct   ☐ incorrect

   _____

2. The anti-pollution criteria for air filters has become much stricter.

   ☐ correct   ☐ incorrect

   _____

3. Neither stricter regulation nor technological development have halted damaging emissions.

   ☐ correct   ☐ incorrect

   _____

4. Stricter regulation, along with heavier fines, has only had a minimal effect.

   ☐ correct   ☐ incorrect

   _____

5. Both of the factories were absolved of any responsibility.

   ☐ correct   ☐ incorrect

   _____

6. The government are increasing funding for non-polluting fuel systems.

   ☐ correct   ☐ incorrect

   _____

Placing the Verb before the Subject

In some sentences, the verb is placed before the subject, for example, with the phrases *there is*, *there are*, *here is*, and *here are*. In such sentences, the verb agrees with the following noun or noun phrase:

Here **is** <u>the exam schedule</u> for the Environmental Sciences class.

Here **are** <u>the exam guidelines</u> for the Environmental Sciences class.

Nouns That Look Plural but Require Singular Verbs

Some nouns look plural but require singular verbs, for example, *news*, fields of study (*mathematics, economics*), expressions of time and distance (*three weeks, five hundred kms*), and amounts of currency (*20 dollars*).

<u>The latest news about improvements in bioprinting</u> **is** promising.

<u>Three weeks</u> **is** a long time to wait for exam results.

<u>Five million dollars</u> **was invested** in bioprinting for regenerative science last year.

Note, however, that plural forms of currency require plural verbs when referring to the *type* of currency:

<u>Euros</u> **are required** in many countries in Europe.

Avoid Common Errors

Be careful to make the verb agree with the subject when you write sentences containing the following structures.

One of the

<u>One of the worst causes of air pollution</u> ~~are~~ **is** nitrogen dioxide.

<u>One of the worst causes of air pollution</u> ~~are~~ **is** nitrogen oxides.

Nouns That Always Require a Plural Verb

<u>The police</u> sometimes ~~arrests~~ **arrest** serious polluters.

<u>People</u> ~~is~~ **are** responsible for recycling their own waste.

A Plural Noun Adjacent to the Verb

<u>My friend who works for two environmental consultants</u> ~~are~~ **is** overworked.

<u>Pollution from coal-fired power plants</u> ~~damage~~ **damages** air quality.

TASK 2

Some of the following sentences have incorrect subject-verb agreement. Identify the incorrect sentences and rewrite them.

1. There's air pollution in most urban areas.

    ☐ correct   ☐ incorrect

2. There's many reasons for governments to invest in recycling.

☐ correct ☐ incorrect

_____

3. The news about the 3D printing for hip transplants were incredible.

☐ correct ☐ incorrect

_____

4. Five million euros have been raised so far for local hospitals.

☐ correct ☐ incorrect

_____

TASK 3

Correct the subject-verb agreement errors in the following paragraph.

3D Printing

One of the most useful technological innovations of recent years have been 3D printing. Everyday household objects, machine parts, and even surgical implants has been constructed by 3D printing. Some experts have gone as far as stating that nothing is impossible with these machines. One of the most beneficial uses of 3D printing are surgical implants. Here is some examples of the types of implants that can be printed three-dimensionally. Recently, in Australia, surgeons successfully implanted a 3D-printed neck vertebra into a patient suffering from cancer. Another common use are dental implants. In fact, several million dollars have been spent on developing these technological advances. International collaboration, as well as local fundraising initiatives, has helped the development of the technology.

_____
_____
_____
_____
_____
_____
_____
_____
_____
_____

My Bookshelf > My eLab >
Exercises > Unit 10

SUBJECT-VERB AGREEMENT

Context	Rule/Explanation	Examples
Basic rules	a) Present-tense verbs, except irregular verbs (e.g., *to be*): the third-person singular form requires an *s*. b) Tenses with auxiliary verbs: only the auxiliary verb agrees with the subject. (Modal auxiliary verbs: No change of form in the third-person singular.)	a) <u>3D printing</u> **involves** using plastic or metal powders to create copies. <u>3D printers</u> **form** thousands of horizontal layers to create objects. b) Recently, <u>air pollution</u> **has damaged** more local environments. <u>Air pollutants</u> **are having** a negative effect on urban life. <u>Pollutant levels in the EU</u> **will fall** further in the future. <u>Air pollution</u> **may rise** further if no action is taken.
Compound subjects made up of two or more nouns or pronouns	a) With *and*: use plural verbs. b) With *or/nor* and singular nouns/pronouns: use singular verbs. c) With *or/nor* and a combination of singular/plural nouns: the verb agrees with the nearest noun/pronoun. d) With *as well as* and *along with*: the verb agrees with the first noun in the subject.	a) <u>Ammonia and nitrogen dioxide</u> **are** two major air pollutants. <u>Pollution, pesticides, and fast food</u> **have been linked** to ill health. b) <u>Fast food or lack of a balanced diet</u> often **leads** to ill health. <u>Neither fast food nor unhealthy eating</u> **explains** why children become ill. c) <u>Fast food or unhealthy eating habits</u> often **lead** to ill health. d) <u>Fast food, along with unhealthy eating,</u> **is** bad for children's health.
Indefinite pronouns	a) Use a singular verb with *another, any-body/one/thing, each, either, every-body/one/thing, neither, nobody, no one, nothing, one, other, some-body/one/thing*. b) Use a plural verb with *both, few, many, others, several*. c) Use either a singular or a plural verb with *all, none,* and *some*.	a) In my opinion, <u>nothing</u> **is** impossible with 3D printing. <u>Something</u> **isn't working** properly in the machine. b) A variety of objects today are made by 3D printing; <u>many</u> **are** prototypes. c) <u>All of the objects on display</u> **were made** with a 3D printer. <u>All of the machinery</u> **is** less than a year old.
Collective nouns	a) Use a singular verb with *class, family, government, team*, etc. b) Use a plural verb when referring to individual members of the group.	a) <u>The Environmental Sciences class</u> **is going** on a field trip next week. b) <u>The Environmental Sciences class</u> **are doing** their individual projects.
Verb before the subject	The verb agrees with the following noun.	Here **is** <u>the exam schedule</u>. Here **are** <u>the exam guidelines</u>.
Nouns that look plural but require singular verbs	a) *news* b) Fields of study (*mathematics*), expressions of time/distance (*three weeks, five hundred kms*), and amounts of money *BUT* c) Types of currency, in the plural, require a plural verb.	a) <u>The latest news about improvements in bioprinting</u> **is** promising. b) <u>Three weeks</u> **is** a long time to wait for exam results. <u>Five million dollars</u> **was invested** in regenerative science last year. c) <u>Euros</u> **are required** in many countries in Europe.
Errors to avoid	a) *One of the . . .* + **singular verb** + singular/plural noun b) *The police/people* + **plural verb** c) Avoid conjugating the verb with the nearest noun.	a) <u>One of the worst causes of air pollution</u> ~~are~~ **is** nitrogen dioxide. <u>One of the worst causes of air pollution</u> ~~are~~ **is** nitrogen oxides. b) <u>The police</u> sometimes ~~arrests~~ **arrest** serious polluters. c) <u>My friend who works for two environmental consultants</u> ~~are~~ **is** overworked.

CONDITIONAL SENTENCES

Conditional sentences have two clauses: the main clause and the conditional clause (also known as the *if clause*). In a conditional sentence, the action or state in the main clause will occur only if a condition in the *if* clause is met. To understand and use conditional sentences correctly, answer the following three questions:

- **Concept:** Is the action or state real or imaginary, possible or impossible?
- **Time idea:** Is the time idea past, present, future, or any time?
- **Form:** How are verb tenses used in the two clauses?

There are three main types of conditional sentence: first, second, and third conditional. In addition, there is a form called the *zero conditional*, and there are combinations of mixed conditionals.

Zero Conditional

In zero-conditional sentences, the action in the main clause always happens. This conditional form is used for factual statements:

> If international students **take** courses at Central University, they **pay** higher tuition fees.

Concept: Factual reality

Time idea: Any time

Verb forms: Present tense (*if* clause) and present tense (main clause)

In the example above, the writer believes that all international students always pay higher tuition fees if they take courses at the university.

First Conditional

The first conditional is used for real possibilities:

> If the college **implements** its mobile learning strategy, most students **will be** pleased.

Concept: Real possibility

Time idea: Present to future

Verb forms: Present tense (*if* clause) and future tense (main clause)

In the example of the first conditional, the writer believes that the actions or states in the two clauses have a real chance of occurring. This statement would be appropriate in the context of a college that has consulted students about introducing mobile learning, leading students to believe it is a real possibility.

Second Conditional

The second conditional is used for imaginary, hypothetical actions and states:

> If the college **implemented** a mobile learning plan, most students **would be** pleased.

Concept: Imaginary, hypothetical reality

Time idea: Present to future

Verb forms: Past tense (*if* clause) and *would* + base form of the verb (main clause)

The second-conditional sentence has the same time idea as the first-conditional example on the preceding page. However, the writer is thinking hypothetically, imagining what would happen if the college were to introduce a mobile learning plan. This statement matches the context of a college that students feel has no stated intention of introducing mobile learning.

> Note that the standard second-conditional form of the verb *to be* is *were* for all persons, including *if I were* and *if he/she/it were*.

Third Conditional

The third conditional is used for ideas about changing the past, which is impossible:

> If my college **had provided** more courses, I **would have graduated** in four instead of six years.

Concept: Impossible reality

Time idea: Past

Verb forms: Past perfect (*if* clause) and *would have* + past participle (main clause)

The writer is looking back at her college years and wondering why it took six years to graduate. She comes to the conclusion that the college did not provide enough courses, hence the statement. The third conditional is often used when people look back on the past and imagine how things might have been different.

TASK 1

Read the following conditional sentences and answer the questions that follow.

1. If you don't study, you fail.

    a) Is the speaker presenting failure as a possible result of not studying or as a factual consequence?

    _____

    b) Is the sentence a zero or first conditional? _____

    c) Does the statement read as encouragement or as a warning?

    _____

2. If you don't study hard, you'll fail.

    a) Does the speaker believe not studying and failure are possible or imaginary?

    _____

b) Is the sentence a first or second conditional? _____

c) Would the speaker be more likely to say this to a good or bad student?

_____

3. If you studied harder, you'd pass.

a) Does the speaker believe studying harder and passing are possible or imaginary?

_____

b) Is the sentence a first or second conditional? _____

c) Would the speaker be more likely to say this to a good or bad student?

_____

4. If I had studied harder, I would have passed with an A.

a) Is the speaker describing a situation that is possible or impossible to change?

_____

b) Is the sentence a second or third conditional? _____

c) Do you think the speaker is looking back with regret or imagining future possibilities?

_____

Mixed Conditionals

It is also possible, and quite common, to mix the *unreal* second and third conditional forms by combining an idea of impossible past with an imaginary present or future.

Combining Impossible Past with Imaginary Present

In the sentences below, the speaker is imagining how, if things had been different in the past (third conditional in the *if* clause), he or she would have more job opportunities in the present (second conditional in the main clause).

> If I **had studied** foreign languages at university, I**'d be** more employable now.
>
> I**'d be** more employable now if I **had studied** foreign languages at university.

Combining Impossible Past with Imaginary Future

In the sentences below, the speaker is imagining how, if things had been different in the past (third conditional in the *if* clause), he or she would be able to start a new job in the future (second conditional in the main clause).

> If I **had studied** foreign languages at university, I think I**'d be starting** a job in Paris next month.
>
> I think I**'d be starting** a job in Paris next month if I **had studied** foreign languages at university.

If the *if* clause comes second in a conditional sentence, there is no comma before *if*.

Alternative Conditional Forms

Modal Auxiliary Verbs

It is possible to replace the auxiliary verbs in the main clause of first, second, and third conditionals with one of the four modal auxiliary verbs *may*, *might*, *could* or *should* to add a more nuanced sense of possibility or probability.

In first-conditional sentences, the use of *should* (sentence 1) adds a sense of future probability and positive expectation. The use of *may*, *might*, and *could* (sentences 2 and 3) adds a sense of present or future possibility.

1. If the college adopts mobile learning, most students **should** be pleased.
2. If the college adopts mobile learning, some students **may**/**might** be pleased.
3. If the college adopts mobile learning, it **could** have positive results.

In second-conditional sentences, the use of *might* and *could* adds a sense of present or future possibility:

> If the college gave more tutorial support, more students **might**/**could** pass their exams.

In third-conditional sentences, the use of *might* and *could* adds a sense of past possibility. Note that it is not possible to use *should* in the main clause of a third-conditional sentence to express past probability.

> If my college had provided more courses, I **might**/**could** have graduated in four instead of six years.

When, As Soon As, and Unless

Another variation of conditional sentences involves replacing *if* with *when*, *as soon as*, or *unless* in first-conditional sentences.

1. **When** the college adopts mobile learning, most students will be pleased.
2. **As soon as** m-learning is adopted, students will need to have smart phones.
3. **Unless** the college adopts mobile learning, exam results will continue to fall.

In sentence 1, the use of *when* suggests that mobile learning is *definitely* going to be adopted. In sentence 2, *as soon as* adds the idea that students will need to have smart phones *immediately after* the policy is implemented. In sentence 3, the use of *unless* means "if not": "if the college does not adopt mobile learning."

Should Instead of If

In first-conditional sentences, *should* can replace *if* to add a sense of formality:

1. **If** you require any assistance, please feel free to ask.
2. **Should** you require any assistance, please feel free to ask.

Sentence 2 is more formal than sentence 1. This form is often used in formal documents and letters.

Were and Was

In second-conditional sentences, *were* and *was* can be used in the *if* clause. *Were* is the standard form; *was* is informal.

> If I **were** you, I would make use of the Student Learning Office.

> If I **was** you, I would make use of the Student Learning Office.

Were To and Was To

In second-conditional sentences, *were to* and *was to* can also be used in the *if* clause:

1. If I graduated in three years, I would be amazed.
2. If I **were to** graduate in three years, I would be amazed.
3. If I **was to** graduate in three years, I would be amazed.

Sentence 1 is the most common form of second conditional, using the past-tense verb. Sentences 2 and 3 have the same meaning as sentence 1; the use of *were* in sentence 2 is standard while *was* in sentence 3 is informal.

Had I and If I Had

It is possible to use *had I/you/we/etc.*, instead of *if I/you/we/etc. had*, in third-conditional if clauses:

1. **If I had** studied foreign languages at university, I'd be more employable now.
2. **Had I** studied foreign languages at university, I'd be more employable now.

Sentences 1 and 2 have the same meaning. The use of *had I* in sentence 2 adds formality.

TASK 2

Follow the prompts and write a corresponding conditional sentence.

1. **Third conditional:** You are looking back and wondering how your life would have been different if you hadn't learned English as a child.

   _____

   _____

2. **Mixed conditional:** You are looking back and wondering what you would be doing now if you hadn't learned English as a child.

   _____

   _____

3. **Second conditional:** You are imagining how your life would be if you had to give up access to mobile devices for one month.

   _____

   _____

4. **Second conditional:** You are recommending to your boss, who is rather formal, to focus more on enjoying life and less on work.

   _____

   _____

5. **Second conditional:** You are recommending to your best friend to focus more on work and less on enjoying life.

_____

_____

6. **Zero conditional:** Explain what happens if you drop a smart phone in water.

_____

_____

7. **Second conditional:** Ask a group of colleagues how they would be affected if they gave up using their cellphones for one month; use _were to_.

_____

_____

8. **First conditional:** Explain to your friend that his or her smart phone will work better immediately after upgrading the operating system; use _as soon as_.

_____

_____

9. **First conditional:** Tell your classmates that they need to share ideas for the group project to get a good grade; use _unless_.

_____

_____

10. Explain to your friend that his or her smart phone will probably work better if he or she upgrades the operating system; you are optimistic.

_____

_____

11. Explain to your friend that his or her smart phone will possibly work better if he or she upgrades the operating system; you are not sure.

_____

_____

12. Advise your friend to change service provider to get better coverage on his or her phone; use _if I were you_.

_____

_____

TASK 3

Practise using the different conditional forms you have learned in this unit by answering at least five of the questions below in a short paragraph.

1. When you look back at your previous studies, do you have any regrets?
2. When you graduate from your planned studies, what do you think you are likely to do next?
3. What would you love to do after graduating, but you think it is an unrealistic hope?
4. What do you plan to do immediately after class today?
5. What reassurance did your family give you recently for your future studies?
6. What warnings did they give you about your studies?
7. What will possibly happen if you pass your academic writing course with a top grade?
8. What do you think will probably happen during your first year at university?

_____

_____

_____

_____

_____

_____

_____

_____

_____

_____

_____

SUMMARY CONDITIONAL SENTENCES

Type of Conditional	Concept/Form	Examples
Zero conditional	**Concept:** Factual reality **Time idea:** Any time **Verb forms:** Present tense and present tense	If international students **take** courses at Central University, they **pay** higher tuition fees.
First conditional	**Concept:** Real possibility **Time idea:** Present to future **Verb forms:** Present tense and future tense	If the college **implements** its mobile learning strategy, most students **will be** pleased.
Second conditional	**Concept:** Imaginary, hypothetical reality **Time idea:** Present to future **Verb forms:** Past tense and *would* + base form of the verb	If the college **implemented** a mobile learning plan, most students **would be** pleased. If mobile learning **were** of use to me, I **would get** a smart phone.

Type of Conditional	Concept/Form	Examples
Third conditional	**Concept:** Impossible reality **Time idea:** Past **Verb forms:** Past perfect and *would have* + past participle	If my college **had provided** more courses, I **would have graduated** in four instead of six years.
Mixed conditionals	a) Impossible past (third conditional) + imaginary present (second conditional) b) Impossible past (third conditional) + imaginary future (second conditional)	a) If I **had studied** foreign languages at university, I**'d be** more employable now. b) If I **had studied** foreign languages at university, I think I**'d be starting** a job in Paris next month.
Alternative Conditional Forms		
First conditional + modal auxiliary verbs	a) *Should*: sense of future probability and positive expectation b) & c) *May*, *might*, and *could*: sense of present or future possibility	a) If the college adopts mobile learning, most students **should** be pleased. b) If the college adopts mobile learning, some students **may/might** be pleased. c) If the college adopts mobile learning, it **could** have positive results.
Second conditional + modal auxiliary verbs	*Might* and *could*: sense of present or future possibility	If the college gave more tutorial support, more students **might/could** pass their exams.
Third conditional + modal auxiliary verbs	*Might* and *could*: sense of past possibility Note: It is not possible to use *should* in the main clause of a third-conditional sentence.	If my college had provided more courses, I **might/could** have graduated in four instead of six years.
First conditional with *when*, *as soon as*, and *unless*	a) *When*: suggestion that event is **definitely** going to happen b) *As soon as*: idea that event will happen **immediately** c) *Unless*: same meaning as "if not"	a) **When** the college adopts mobile learning, most students will be pleased. b) **As soon as** m-learning is adopted, students will need to have smart phones. c) **Unless** the college adopts mobile learning, exam results will continue to fall.
First conditional with *should*	• More formal than with *if* • Often used in formal documents and letters	**Should** you require any assistance, please feel free to ask. (**If** you require any assistance, . . .)
Second conditional with *was*	• Less formal than *were* • Non-standard form	If I **was** you, I would make use of the Student Learning Office. (If I **were** you, . . .)
Second conditional with *were/was to*	• Same meaning as the more usual form with past-tense verb: "If I graduated in three years, . . ." • The use of *were to* adds formality.	a) If I **were to** graduate in three years, I would be amazed. b) If I **was to** graduate in three years, I would be amazed.
Third conditional with *had I*	More formal than *if I had*	**Had I** studied foreign languages at university, I'd be more employable now. (**If I had** studied foreign languages at university, . . .)

PARALLEL STRUCTURE

The term parallel structure (also known as *parallelism*) refers to the use of the same types of words and phrases by writers when they provide a series of items or examples in a sentence. In academic writing, the use of parallel structure adds cohesion to sentences and accords equal importance to ideas. Consider the examples below:

1. Solar energy is cheap, clean, renewable, and effective. (parallel)
2. Solar energy is cheap, clean, renewable, and delivers power efficiently. (not parallel)

Sentence 1 has parallel structure because each of the four items in the series is an adjective: *cheap*, *clean*, *renewable*, and *effective*. Sentence 2 does not have parallel structure because three of the four items are adjectives (*cheap*, *clean*, *renewable*), but the fourth is a verb phrase (*delivers power efficiently*).

1. Solar power costs less than other energy forms, uses natural energy sources, and delivers power efficiently. (parallel)
2. Solar power has three main benefits: it costs less than other energy forms, uses natural energy sources, and efficient power delivery. (not parallel)

Sentence 1 has parallel structure because each of the three benefits includes a verb: **costs** *less than other energy forms*, **uses** *natural energy sources*, and **delivers** *power efficiently*. Sentence 2 does not have parallel structure because the first two benefits include verbs while the third is a noun phrase: *efficient power delivery*.

Different Forms of Parallel Structure

The following are the most common parts of a sentence that may, or may not, form parallel structures.

Adjectives and Adverbs

1. Solar energy is **cheap**, **clean**, **renewable**, and **effective**. (parallel)
2. The new wind power policy was implemented **quickly**, **fairly**, and **efficiently**. (parallel)
3. The new wind power policy was implemented **fairly**, **efficiently**, and **in two years**. (not parallel)

Sentence 1 has parallel structure because each item is an adjective. Sentence 2 also has parallel structure because each item is a single-word adverb. Sentence 3 does not have parallel structure because two single-word adverbs are followed by a preposition phrase: *in two years*.

Gerunds and Infinitives

1. Nuclear energy is often applauded for **reducing** carbon emissions, **providing** a reliable energy supply, and **cutting** fuel bills. (parallel)
2. All energy providers aim to **reduce** carbon emissions, **provide** a reliable energy supply, and **cut** fuel bills. (parallel)
3. Nuclear energy is often applauded for **reducing** carbon emissions, **the provision** of reliable energy, and **because it cuts fuel bills**. (not parallel)

The structure is parallel in sentences 1 and 2 because the actions are expressed as gerunds and infinitives, respectively. The structure of sentence 3 is not parallel because the actions are expressed as a gerund, a noun phrase, and a clause.

Verbs Followed by a Gerund or an Infinitive

When a verb can be followed by either a gerund or an infinitive, keep the structure parallel.

1. Due to public pressure, energy suppliers began **consulting** with local communities, **implementing** environmental audits, and **promoting** the benefits of cheap energy. (parallel)
2. Due to public pressure, energy suppliers began to **consult** with local communities, **implement** environmental audits, and **promote** the benefits of cheap energy. (parallel)
3. Due to public pressure, energy suppliers began **consulting** with local communities, **implementing** environmental audits, and **to promote** the benefits of cheap energy. (not parallel)

Sentences 1 and 2 have parallel structure because they contain series of gerunds and infinitives, respectively. The structure of sentence 3 is not parallel because the series contains two gerunds, followed by an infinitive: *to promote*.

Verb Phrases

1. Solar power **costs less than other energy forms**, **uses natural energy sources**, and **delivers power efficiently**. (parallel)
2. Solar power is popular because it **uses natural energy sources**, **delivers power efficiently**, and **for its low long-term costs**. (not parallel)

Sentence 1 has parallel structure because each item is a verb phrase. Sentence 2 does not have parallel structure because the first two items are verb phrases while the third is a preposition phrase: *for its low long-term costs*.

TASK 1

Indicate whether the structure of the following sentences is parallel or not. Underline any words, phrases, or clauses that break the parallel structure.

1. Solar energy requires large areas of land, produces power intermittently, and takes time to yield financial returns.

   ☐ parallel   ☐ not parallel

2. Solar energy is environmentally friendly, renewable, and does not pollute the air.

   ☐ parallel   ☐ not parallel

A gerund is a verb + *ing* that functions as a noun in a sentence, and an infinitive is the form of a verb that follows *to*.

3. The new wind power station was set up within three years, built on budget, and welcomed by the local community.

   ☐ parallel ☐ not parallel

4. This proves that wind power can be set up quickly, cost-effective, and welcomed by communities.

   ☐ parallel ☐ not parallel

TASK 2

Rewrite any sentences that do not have parallel structure. Not all of the sentences require changes.

1. Solar energy requires large areas of land, cannot produce power continuously, and is slow to yield financial returns.

   _____

   _____

2. The new wind power station was set up within three years, popular with the local community, and built on budget.

   _____

   _____

3. Solar power has three main benefits: it is more carbon-friendly than other energy forms, it does not pollute the air, and its popularity with the public.

   _____

   _____

4. The new-generation nuclear power station was built quickly, fairly, and efficiently.

   _____

   _____

5. The energy produced from the nuclear power plant will reduce carbon emissions, provide a reliable energy supply, and cut fuel bills.

   _____

   _____

6. The owners of the plant have three key aims: to provide power to hundreds of thousands of homes, to meet government production targets, and low carbon emissions.

   _____

   _____

7. Solar panels are cheap, efficient, and do not harm the environment.

_____

_____

8. Many environmentalist groups are known for opposing nuclear energy, promoting solar power, and their support for other renewable sources.

_____

_____

My Bookshelf > My eLab >
Exercises > Unit 12

TASK 3

When you have finished the first draft of the writing task for Chapter 12 (see p. 264), reread your draft to look for parallel structure, or lack of it. You can do this by looking specifically for series of items and for keywords such as *and* and *or.* Correct any sentences that lack parallel structure.

SUMMARY   PARALLEL STRUCTURE

Parts of the Sentence	Parallel Examples	Non-Parallel Example with Explanation
Adjectives and adverbs	Solar energy is **cheap**, **clean**, **renewable**, and **effective**. The new wind power policy was implemented **quickly**, **fairly**, and **efficiently**.	The new wind power policy was implemented **fairly**, **efficiently**, and **in two years**. The structure is not parallel because two single-word adverbs are followed by a preposition phrase: *in two years*.
Gerunds and infinitives	Nuclear energy is often applauded for **reducing carbon emissions**, **providing a reliable energy supply**, and **cutting fuel bills**. All energy providers aim to **reduce carbon emissions**, **provide a reliable energy supply**, and **cut fuel bills**.	Nuclear energy is often applauded for **reducing carbon emissions**, **the provision of reliable energy**, and **because it cuts fuel bills**. The structure is not parallel because the items in the series are a gerund, a noun phrase, and a clause.
Verbs followed by a gerund or an infinitive	Due to public pressure, energy suppliers began **consulting** with local communities, **implementing** environmental audits, and **promoting** the benefits of cheap energy. Due to public pressure, energy suppliers began to **consult** with local communities, **implement** environmental audits, and **promote** the benefits of cheap energy.	Due to public pressure, energy suppliers began **consulting** with local communities, **implementing** environmental audits, and **to promote** the benefits of cheap energy. The structure is not parallel because two gerunds are followed by an infinitive: *to promote*. When a verb can be followed by either a gerund or an infinitive, keep the structure parallel.
Verb phrases	Solar power **costs less than other energy forms**, **uses natural energy sources**, and **delivers power efficiently**.	Solar power is popular because it **uses natural energy sources**, **delivers power efficiently**, and **for its low long-term costs**. The structure is not parallel because two verb phrases are followed by a preposition phrase: *for its low long-term costs*.

MODAL AUXILIARY VERBS TO EXPRESS LIKELIHOOD AND OBLIGATION

Modality

Modal auxiliary verbs express different aspects of modality. The term *modality* refers to the attitude of writers or speakers when they are describing things. Common aspects of modality that are expressed with modal auxiliary verbs are likelihood, obligation, ability, permission, willingness, and necessity.

Other words and phrases in the English language also express modality; for example, *have to* and *ought to* can be used to express obligation. Although some linguists claim that such phrases are not modal auxiliary verbs, they are included in this unit in cases where they express degrees of modality.

When you write different types of essays, you need to express if you think things are possible, probable, or certain, and whether there is a strong or mild obligation for people or organizations to do things.

In this unit, the focus is on modal auxiliary verbs that express likelihood and obligation. Remember that when writers or speakers express likelihood and obligation, they are expressing their attitude: whether they think something is, was, or will be possible, probable, or certain; and whether they believe that there is a strong or mild sense of obligation for something to happen.

Two Ways to Express Attitude

There are always two or more ways to write a sentence expressing modality. In the following examples, sentence 1 expresses likelihood or obligation using a modal auxiliary verb, and sentence 2 expresses the same idea in other terms.

Likelihood: Possibility

1. The government's new policies **may/might/could** protect linguistic minorities.
2. **I think** the government's new policies **will possibly** protect linguistic minorities.

Likelihood: Probability (with Positive or Optimistic Expectation)

1. The government's new policies **should** be successful.
2. **I think** the government's new policies **will probably** be successful.

Mild Obligation

1. Schools **should** do more to help students from all minority backgrounds.
2. **I believe** schools **have an obligation to** do more to help students from all minority backgrounds.

Strong Obligation

1. Schools **must** do more to help students from all minority backgrounds.
2. **I strongly believe** schools **have an obligation to** do more to help students from all minority backgrounds.

The examples above illustrate three important points to remember about modal auxiliary verbs:

1. There are always alternative ways of expressing modality.
2. Modal auxiliary verbs represent the subjective attitude of the speaker.
3. The same modal auxiliary verb can express different aspects of modality. For example, in the sentences above, *should* is used to express probability as well as mild obligation.

MODALITY | LIKELIHOOD

Use the following modal auxiliary verbs to express degrees of likelihood. Affirmative sentences are indicated by a + and negative sentences, by a −.

I'm Certain . . .

Will

Time Idea	Examples
Present	Who's texting you? + That **will be** my boss asking where I am. − It **won't be** my boss. She's on holiday this week.
Future	+ If someone calls later, it**'ll be** my boss. Tell her I'm on my way. − If someone calls later, it **won't be** my boss. She's on holiday this week.
Past	Someone called last night. + That **will have been** my boss. I was running late. − It **won't have been** my boss. She never calls at night.

Will is used in the examples above to express certainty. The certainty is based on the speaker's knowledge of the habits, routines, and characteristics of her boss.

Must

Time Idea	Examples
Present	Someone's at the door. + That **must be** my roommate. − That **can't be** my roommate.
Future	There is no future form of *must* for certainty.

Time Idea	Examples
Past	Someone called last night. + It **must have been** my roommate. – It **can't/couldn't have been** my roommate.

Must is used in the examples above to express certainty. Unlike *will*, *must* gives no indication of knowledge of others' habits, routines, and characteristics.

I Think It's Probable . . .

Should

Time Idea	Examples
Present	+ The projector **should be working**. Let's check. – There ***shouldn't be** any problems. The projector is brand new.
Future	+ You **should pass** the exam tomorrow. I'm confident you're ready. – You ***shouldn't have** any problems tomorrow. Be confident!
Past	+ You ***should have passed** the exam. What went wrong? – You ***shouldn't have failed** the exam. What went wrong?

Should is used in the examples above to express probability. The use of *should* for probability expresses an idea of positive or optimistic expectation. Avoid using it in other contexts; for example, if you thought that a friend is probably going to fail his exam, and you said "You should fail," it would sound like you wanted him to fail! Also note the examples marked by an asterisk (*). These examples could be misinterpreted because *should* is also used to express obligation.

I Think It's Possible . . .

May, Might, and Could

Time Idea	Examples
Present	+ You **may/might/could be** in the wrong classroom. Have you checked your planner? – The exam **may/might not be** in this building. Can you check your planner for me?
Future	+ You **may/might/could pass** the exam tomorrow. I think you have a chance. – You **may/might not pass** the exam tomorrow. Prepare yourself.
Past	+ You **may/might/could have passed** the exam, but you won't know your grade until the end of term. – You **may/might not have passed** the exam, so you should work hard on your term paper.

May, *might*, and *could* are used in the examples above to express possibility in the affirmative for all time ideas. However, only *may* and *might* can be used in the negative forms, not *could*. The three forms have similar degrees of certainty. *May* is the most common form used in academic writing as it carries a sense of formality.

TASK 1

Fill in the blanks in the sentences below with modal auxiliary verbs that express likelihood. Decide whether the form should be affirmative or negative and whether the time idea is present, future, or past. Use the verbs (and adverbs) in brackets, and follow the prompts in parentheses.

1. It _____ [be] easy moving to another country as an international student. (I'm sure it wasn't.)

2. You _____ [miss] your friends and family. (I'm certain you are.)

3. Working for a few years _____ [also be] an option. (I think it would have been possible.)

4. You _____ [experience] any problems getting used to life as a student here and succeeding in your studies. (I'm optimistic: I think it's probable that you won't.)

5. You _____ [even decide] to live and work here for a few years after you graduate. (I think it will be possible.)

MODALITY ## OBLIGATION

Use the modal auxiliary verbs below, and the following phrases, to express degrees of obligation. Affirmative sentences are indicated by a + and negative sentences, by a −.

Strong Sense of Obligation

Must

Time Idea	Examples
Present	+ You **must focus** more. I'm trying to explain! − You **don't have to study** much because you're so clever! − Students ***mustn't bring / aren't allowed to bring** phones into the exam room.
Future	+ You **must study** harder next year. − You **don't/won't have to study** harder next year. − Students ***mustn't bring / won't be allowed to bring** phones into the exam room tomorrow.
Past	+ I **had to study** hard, but I passed! − I **didn't have to study** much. It was easy. − Students ***weren't allowed to bring** phones into the exam room.

Must is used in the affirmative examples above to express strong obligation for present and future time. The affirmative form of *must* in the past tense is *had to*.

© ERPI Reproduction prohibited

Use *have to* for most negative sentences; *mustn't* is used in the negative form only when something is forbidden, as illustrated in the examples marked with an asterisk. Use *mustn't* or *not allowed to* for prohibition in the present and future, but only *wasn't/weren't allowed to* in the past.

Have To

Time Idea	Examples
Present	+ You **have to pay attention** to this. You need to know it to pass the quiz.
	− You **don't have to study** much to get good grades. You're so lucky!
Future	+ You **(will) have to study** hard next year if you want to get a scholarship.
	− You **don't/won't have to improve** your grades next year to keep the scholarship.
Past	+ I **had to study** hard, but I passed!
	− I **didn't have to study** much. It was easy.

The use of *have to* in the examples above expresses strong obligation, as does *must* in the previous examples. However, there is a difference between the sense of obligation in *must* and *have to* in some cases, as the following sentences illustrate:

1. You **must focus** more. I'm trying to explain! (internal obligation)
2. You **have to pay attention** to this for the scholarship. (external obligation)

In sentence 1, the speaker uses *must* to emphasize that the obligation is internal; in other words, it is up to the person being addressed to make the effort to focus more. In sentence 2, the speaker uses *have to* because the obligation is external to the person; it comes from an external source: the scholarship requirements.

Mild Sense of Obligation

Should

Time Idea	Examples
Present	+ Schools **should do** more to support minority languages.
	+ You ***should consider** getting a private tutor for help.
	− Schools **shouldn't spend** so much time on formal assessment.
	− You ***shouldn't waste** money on a private tutor.
Future	+ Schools **should increase** their budgets for teaching assistants next year.
	+ You ***should live** near the campus when you start college in September.
	− Schools **shouldn't reduce** their budgets for teaching assistants next year.
	− You ***shouldn't live** far from the campus when you start college in September.
Past	+ The school **should have done** more to support its international students.
	+ You ***should have considered** getting a private tutor for help.
	− The school **shouldn't have focused** so much on formal assessment.
	− You ***shouldn't have wasted** your money on a private tutor.

Should is used in the sentences above to express mild obligation. The negative *shouldn't* and the past form *should have* are used consistently, without changes in meaning. The sentences marked with an asterisk express recommendation.

TASK 2

Fill in the blanks in the sentences below with modal auxiliary verbs that express obligation. Decide whether the form should be affirmative or negative and whether the time idea is present, future, or past. Use the verbs in brackets, and follow the prompts in parentheses.

1. I _____ [study] harder! (It's up to me to achieve this.)

2. I _____ [maintain] a B average to keep my scholarship. (It's a requirement of the scholarship.)

3. Next term, I _____ [take] four courses. I have no choice. (It's a condition of the program.)

4. Students _____ [smoke] inside any building. It's the law. (The law forbids smoking inside buildings.)

5. Now that I'm living on campus, I _____ [take] the bus to class every day. (I can walk.)

6. Last week, I _____ [prepare] for two mid-term exams. (The mid-terms were compulsory.)

7. You _____ [take] too many courses during your first term. (I'm making a recommendation.)

Other Ways to Express Obligation

Need To

Need to is used to express necessity. It is often used as an alternative to *have to* when there is little difference in meaning between necessity and obligation. The examples below show the different forms of *need to*.

Time Idea	Examples
Present	+ You **need to ask** someone to lend you their lecture notes. – You **don't need to ask** anyone for extra help. You're doing fine. – You ***needn't ask** anyone for extra help. You're doing fine.
Future	+ You **(will) need to take** the bus to the downtown campus tomorrow. – I **won't/don't need to ask** for a ride to the downtown campus tomorrow. – I ***needn't ask** for a ride to the downtown campus tomorrow.
Past	+ I **needed to ask** for a ride to the campus this morning. There were no buses. – You **needn't have given** me a ride to campus. I could have walked. Thanks, though. – He **didn't need to give** me a ride to campus. I walked.

Need to is used in the present and future forms and means "it is / will be necessary" and "it isn't / won't be necessary." The negative form *needn't* is marked with an asterisk because it is less common and rather old-fashioned. In the past negative form, there is an important distinction to note between *needn't have* and *didn't need to*: use *needn't have* when something took place but was unnecessary; use *didn't need to* when something did not take place and was unnecessary.

She gave me a ride ⟶ You **needn't have given** me a ride to campus.

He didn't give me a ride ⟶ He **didn't need to give** me a ride to campus.

Ought To

Ought to can be used as an alternative to *should* for likelihood and obligation. The negative form of *ought to* is *ought not (to)* or *oughtn't (to)*. The past forms are *ought to have* and *ought not (to) have*. *Ought to* is more common in British English and often seems rather old-fashioned and formal. The negative and past forms are not commonly used in modern English.

+ You **ought to pass** the exam. (I think it's probable, and I'm hopeful.)

+ Schools **ought to do** more to support minority languages. (I think it is their duty.)

Have Got To

Have got to is commonly used, especially in British English, as a less formal alternative to *have to*. The negative forms are *hasn't/haven't got to*. The past forms are *had to* and *didn't have to*.

+ You **have got to pay attention** to this. You need to know it to pass the quiz.

– You **haven't got to study** much to get good grades. You're so lucky!

+ I **had to** study so hard!

– You **didn't have to** study much. Lucky you!

TASK 3

Rewrite the paragraph below about a student's life during the first term of a new degree program. Use modal auxiliary verbs and phrases of likelihood and obligation that you have studied in this unit. Focus on the underlined words, which express modality.

When I got a call at 8:00 last night, I said to myself, "I'm certain that is my parents calling as they always call at this time on a Sunday." They wanted to know how I was and reminded me that I am required to maintain a B average as a condition of my student visa. They also said it was up to me to be focused and organized and that no one else can help me with that. I am certain that my parents are missing me a lot and want to come to visit. It is probable (and I hope) that they will be able to visit me during spring break next year. If so, I'm certain they won't have as bad a time as they did when they visited my brother at college last year. When they bought their tickets to Los Angeles, the travel agent forgot to tell them that it was necessary for them to have a biometric passport to get into the country. <u>I think it would have been a good idea for them to have checked</u> because when they tried to check in at the airport, they were told that <u>they were prohibited from boarding</u> the plane with their old-style passports. They missed the flight!

_____

_____

_____

_____

_____

_____

_____

_____

_____

_____

_____

My Bookshelf > My eLab >
Exercises > Unit 13

MODAL AUXILIARY VERBS TO EXPRESS LIKELIHOOD

Time Idea	Examples	Explanation
Certainty		
Present	Who's texting you? + That **will be** my boss asking where I am. − That **won't be** my boss. She's on holiday this week.	***Will*** is used to express certainty based on the speaker's knowledge of the habits, routines, and characteristics of her boss.
Future	+ If someone calls later, it**'ll be** my boss. Tell her I'm on my way. − If someone calls later, it **won't be** my boss. She's on holiday this week.	
Past	Someone called last night. + That **will have been** my boss. I was running late. − It **won't have been** my boss. She never calls at night.	
Present	Someone's at the door. + That **must be** my roommate. − That **can't be** my roommate.	***Must*** is used to express certainty. Unlike *will*, the use of *must* gives no indication of the speaker's knowledge of the habits, routines, and characteristics of her roommate.
Future	There is no future form of *must* for certainty.	
Past	Someone called last night. + It **must have been** my roommate. − It **can't/couldn't have been** my roommate.	

Time Idea	Examples	Explanation
	Probability	
Present	+ The projector **should be working**. Let's check. − There ***shouldn't be** any problems. The projector is brand new.	**Should** is used to express probability. The use of *should* for probability carries an idea of positive, optimistic expectation. The examples marked by an asterisk could be misinterpreted as mild obligation.
Future	+ You **should pass** the exam tomorrow. I'm confident you're ready. − You ***shouldn't have** any problems tomorrow. Be confident!	
Past	+ You ***should have passed** the exam. What went wrong? − You ***shouldn't have failed** the exam. What went wrong?	
	Possibility	
Present	+ You **may/might/could be** in the wrong classroom. Have you checked your planner? − The exam **may/might not be** in this building. Can you check, please?	**May**, **might**, and **could** express possibility in the affirmative for all time ideas. For possibility, only *may* and *might* can be used in the negative forms, not *could*. The three forms have similar degrees of certainty. *May* is the most common form used in academic writing as it carries a sense of formality.
Future	+ You **may/might/could pass** the exam tomorrow. You have a chance. − You **may/might not pass** the exam tomorrow. Prepare yourself.	
Past	+ You **may/might/could have passed** the exam, but you won't know your grade until the end of term. − You **may/might not have passed** the exam, so you should work hard on your term paper.	

SUMMARY

MODAL AUXILIARY VERBS TO EXPRESS OBLIGATION

Time Idea	Examples	Explanation
	Strong Obligation	
Present	+ You **must focus** more. I'm trying to explain! − You **don't have to study** much because you're so clever! − Students ***mustn't bring / aren't allowed to bring** phones into the exam room.	**Must** expresses strong obligation in the present and future; the affirmative form of *must* in the past is *had to*. Use *have to* for negative sentences. *Mustn't* is used only when something is forbidden: see the examples marked with an asterisk. Use only *wasn't/weren't allowed to* for prohibition in the past.
Future	+ You **must study** harder next year. − You **don't/won't have to study** harder next year. − Students ***mustn't bring / won't be allowed to bring** phones into the exam room tomorrow.	
Past	+ I **had to study** hard, but I passed! − I **didn't have to study** much. It was easy. − Students ***weren't allowed to bring** phones into the exam room.	
Present	+ You **have to pay attention**. You need to know this for the quiz. − You **don't have to study** much to get good grades. You're lucky!	**Have to** expresses strong obligation, as does *must*.
Future	+ You **(will) have to study** hard next year to get a scholarship. − You **don't/won't have to improve** your grades next year to keep the scholarship.	
Past	+ I **had to study** hard, but I passed! − I **didn't have to study** much. It was easy.	

Time Idea	Examples	Explanation
	Internal versus External Obligation	
	a) You **must focus** more. I'm trying to explain!	a) The obligation is internal: it is up to the person being addressed to become more focused.
	b) You **have to pay attention** to this for the scholarship.	b) The obligation is external: it comes from the scholarship requirements.
	Mild Obligation	
Present	+ Schools **should do** more to support minority languages. + You ***should consider** getting a private tutor for help. – Schools **shouldn't spend** so much time on formal assessment. – You ***shouldn't waste** money on a private tutor.	**Should** expresses mild obligation, without changes in meaning in the negative and past forms *shouldn't* and *should have*.
Future	+ Schools **should increase** their budgets for TAs next year. + You ***should live** near the campus in September. – Schools **shouldn't reduce** their budgets for TAs next year. – You ***shouldn't live** far from the campus in September.	The sentences marked with an asterisk express recommendation.
Past	+ The school **should have done** more for international students. + You ***should have considered** getting a private tutor for help. – The school **shouldn't have focused** so much on assessment. – You ***shouldn't have wasted** your money on a private tutor.	
	Other Forms	
Present	+ You **need to ask** someone to lend you their lecture notes. – You **don't need to ask** anyone for extra help. You're doing fine. – You ***needn't ask** anyone for extra help. You're doing fine.	**Need to** expresses necessity and can be used instead of *have to* for obligation.
Future	+ You **(will) need to take** the bus to the campus tomorrow. – I **won't/don't need to ask** for a ride to the campus tomorrow. – I ***needn't ask** for a ride to the campus tomorrow.	*Needn't* is marked with an asterisk because it is less common and sounds old-fashioned.
Past	+ I **needed to get** a ride from a friend. There were no buses. – You **needn't have given** me a ride. I could have walked. – He **didn't need to give** me a ride to campus. I walked.	Use *needn't have* when something took place but was unnecessary. Use *didn't need to* when something did not take place and was unnecessary.
Present	+ a) You **ought to pass** the exam. + b) Schools **ought to do** more to support minority languages. – a) You **ought not to fail** the exam. – b) Schools **ought not to reduce** their budgets for minority language programs.	**Ought to** means the same as *should* for likelihood (a) and obligation (b). It is more common in British English, and more formal than *should*.
Past	+ a) You **ought to have passed** the exam. What happened? – b) You **ought not to have said** that. He was offended.	The negative and past forms are uncommon in modern English.
Present	+ You **have got to pay attention** to pass the quiz. – You **haven't got to study** much to get good grades. You're lucky!	**Have got to** is common, especially in British English, as a less formal alternative to *have to*.
Past	+ You **had to pay attention** to the questions because the sound quality was poor. – I **didn't have to study** hard for the test. It was easy.	The past forms are the same as for *have to*: *had to*, *didn't have to*.

INVERSION FOR EMPHASIS

It is possible to add emphasis to sentences by adding emphatic adverbs or adverbial phrases at the beginning of the independent clause. These are generally words or phrases that have a negative connotation, and they are usually placed at the beginning of the sentence.

EXPRESSIONS   EMPHATIC ADVERBS

When the following emphatic adverbs (in bold) are placed at the beginning of an independent clause, the usual subject-verb order (underlined) is reversed.

1. **At no time** should residents leave their homes during a tornado.
2. **Hardly** had the rain ended when our home became flooded.
3. **Little** did we know that the storm would last for three days.
4. **Never** have I been so frightened as during that storm.
5. **No sooner** had the rain ended than the heavy winds began.
6. **Not once** did I panic while I was inside my house.
7. **Not only** were trees felled by the winds, (but) local rivers also flooded.
8. **Not since** my childhood have I lived through such extreme weather.
9. **Not until** the weather settled did life return to normal.
10. **Only after** the weather settled did life return to normal.
11. **On no account** should people leave their homes during a tornado.
12. **Rarely** have I witnessed such rain damage.
13. **Seldom** does so much rain fall in one day.
14. **So** heavy was the rain that local rivers broke their banks.
15. **Under no circumstances** should you approach a fallen power line.
16. People living away from the coast were not affected. **Neither** were the people living on higher land.
17. People living away from the coast were not affected. **Nor** were the people living on higher land.

FORM   INVERSION

Three Forms of Inversion

When beginning independent clauses with certain emphatic adverbs, change the subject-verb order in one of the following three ways:

1. When the main verb is *to be*, change the subject-verb order.

   <u>Climate change is</u> the result of both human activity and natural phenomena.

   Not only <u>is climate change</u> the result of human activity, it is also caused by natural phenomena.

2. For verbs with auxiliaries, change the subject-auxiliary order.

   <u>Pacific storms have become</u> so severe that evacuation of communities is now a regular occurrence.

   So severe <u>have Pacific storms become</u> that evacuation of communities is now a regular occurrence.

3. For other verbs, use question structure, with a form of the auxiliary verb *to do*.

   <u>El Niño rarely leaves</u> coastal Pacific communities unscathed.

   Rarely <u>does El Niño leave</u> coastal Pacific communities unscathed.

Forms without Inversion

If the emphatic adverbs listed on page 93 are used within an independent clause that begins with *it is/was*, the subject-verb order in the following dependent clause (*that* …) is not reversed.

Not until the end of the storm <u>did people venture</u> out of their shelters.	(subject-verb order changed)
It was not until the end of the storm that <u>people ventured</u> out of their shelters.	(subject-verb order unchanged)
Only after coastal erosion affected communities <u>was action taken</u>.	(subject-verb order changed)
It was only after coastal erosion affected communities that <u>action was taken</u>.	(subject-verb order unchanged)

Not Only

If the independent clause begins with *not only*, it requires inversion when the writer wishes to emphasize the action of the verb, as in the following example:

   Not only <u>does El Niño damage</u> coastal communities, it also affects people living further inland.

However, in other cases, an independent clause can contain the phrase *not only*, or even begin with it, and yet not require inversion, as illustrated in the following examples:

   <u>El Niño affects</u> **not only** coastal communities **but also** people living further inland.

   Not only coastal communities **but also** <u>people living further inland suffer</u> during El Niño years.

In these examples, there is no inversion because *not only* is not an emphatic adverb that modifies the verb *affects* or *suffer*, but the first part of a correlative conjunction (*not only … but also*) joining two noun phrases: *coastal communities* and *people living further inland*.

> Learn more about correlative conjunctions as linking words in Appendix 1, p. 108.

TASK 1

Rewrite each of the following sentences to add emphasis, beginning with the emphatic adverb in parentheses.

1. People living in the town are not allowed to return until the storm clears. (Under no circumstances)

   _____

   _____

2. The storm damaged many small homes in the area as well as local crops. (Not only)

   _____

   _____

3. Local residents were able to return home two months later. (Only after)

   _____

4. A storm of such intensity had not struck the town since 2005. (Not since)

   _____

5. People living in the town were not allowed to return until the storm had cleared. (Not until)

   _____

6. People with homes in the area should not return without authorization. (At no time)

   _____

7. People with homes in the area should not return until the flooding subsides. (On no account)

   _____

   _____

8. Areas of Argentina and southern Brazil are seldom affected by El Niño-related extreme weather events. (Seldom)

   _____

   _____

9. In all its history, the coastal town has rarely been so badly affected by storms. (Rarely)

   _____

10. The town was so badly affected by the storm that many residents were forced to live in temporary shelters. (So badly)

   _____

   _____

11. People fleeing the flooding had no shelter. They didn't have food either. (Nor)

_____

12. As soon as the storm cleared, people left their homes to assess the damage. (No sooner)

_____

13. As soon as the storm cleared, people left their homes to assess the damage. (Hardly)

_____

14. They were completely unaware that an even stronger storm was on its way. (Little)

_____

15. Local people were not aware that a new storm was on its way. The meteorologists weren't either. (Neither)

_____

_____

16. During my 20 years in the country, I have never experienced such extreme weather. (Not once)

_____

_____

17. Extreme weather has never been so severe as during the last seven years. (Never)

_____

TASK 2

The following sentences are from the results on a search engine when the keywords *extreme weather* were combined with the emphatic adverbs listed on page 93. In the sentences, the adverbs have been replaced with blanks. Fill in each blank with an emphatic adverb that fits conceptually and grammatically. Try to use each adverb only once. In some cases, more than one answer is possible.

1. The signs of climate change are right in front of us, says the assessment's chapter on agriculture, one of the few comprehensive reports to explicitly point to certain events—like the 2012 drought—as an example of the consequences of climate change. _____ will weather affect crop growth, but it will encourage invasive species and pests, lower the quality of forage for livestock and lead to changing land uses across the country, the report says.

(https://www.scientificamerican.com/article/deadly-heat-waves-flooding-rains-crop-failures-among-climate-change-plagues-already-afflicting-americans/)

2. A near-record year for wind events. _____ 2007 have so many storms exceeded gusts of 90 kms per hour and Alberta broke the previous record with 41 wind storms—up from the high of 37 in 2007.

   (http://www.huffingtonpost.ca/2012/12/20/calgary-hail-stor-environment-canadas-top-10-extreme-weather-events_n_2339941.html)

3. As the sea ice melts, sea surface temperatures will remain at around zero degree Celsius (32 °F) for as long as there is ice in the water, since the extra energy will first go into melting the ice. _____ the ice has melted will the extra energy start raising the temperature of the water.

   (http://arctic-news.blogspot.ca/2016/07/extreme-weather-events.html)

4. The Himalayan Mountains have long kept a dark secret. In 1942, hundreds of human skeletons dating back to the 9th century were discovered around an upland lake in northern India. They had all died at the same time. But _____ 2007 did scientists offer an explanation for their mysterious demise. All the bodies showed similar wounds: deep cracks in the skull. Scientists came up with a stunning explanation. They were killed by cricket-ball-sized hailstones.

   (https://www.allianz.com/en/about_us/open-knowledge/topics/environment/articles/130903-hailstorms-threaten-rising-losses.html/)

5. There are many caves and potholes. Unless you are part of a properly equipped, experienced and supervised group, stay well away from them. The substantial quarry on the Southernmost section of the reserve on Moughton Fell is a fully operational site, and _____ should you cross its perimeter. If you hear a siren, it may indicate imminent blasting at the quarry—you should move well away from the boundary.

   (http://www.inclusivelondon.com/information/Ingleborough%20National%20Nature%20Reserve/103010/info/information.aspx)

6. To reduce your chance of encountering a bear: travel in large groups; avoid areas of obvious recent bear activity; avoid carrion (dead meat); camp well inland of the coast or in areas with good visibility in all directions; and cook less odorous food. _____ should you approach a polar bear. If a bear is encountered, noise-makers such as bear bangers and air horns may scare the bear away. Pepper spray, used at close range, may deter polar bears, but it has not been thoroughly tested.

   (http://www.pc.gc.ca/eng/pn-np/nt/aulavik/visit/visit4/a.aspx)

7. I have lived in Australia for 16 years (minus the two I spent wandering the globe), and in all that time _____ did a cyclone even come close to where we live in south-east Queensland. Now we had two bearing down on us, with one showing the possibility of changing that fact very quickly!

(https://onewanderlustlife.wordpress.com/2015/02/23/australian-summer-extreme-weather-edition/)

8. _____ does one hear any working scientist say that science is "settled." Science is never settled. It is, by definition, an ever-evolving body of human knowledge, and climate science is exactly like all the other sciences in that way.

(http://www.nytimes.com/interactive/projects/cp/climate/2015-paris-climate-talks/how-can-science-be-settled)

9. Pagliuca, Stephenson and McKenzie, along with their guests, awoke to a brilliant sunrise early on April 11. The coal stove in the Auto Road's Stage Office (the Observatory's early home) took the chill off the room. " _____ did we realize as we were enjoying a fine view of the Atlantic Ocean that we were to experience during the next 48 hours one of the worst storms ever recorded in the history of any observatory."
—Log Book entry, Sal Pagliuca

(https://www.mountwashington.org/about-us/history/world-record-wind.aspx)

10. Air France said it had cancelled 210 flights and booked more than 2,000 hotel rooms for its stranded passengers. At sea, the ferry services connecting the northwestern department of Brittany with nearby islands were all suspended—and the inaugural voyage of the Roscoff-Plymouth ferry service was post-poned. _____ bad was the weather that northeastern France was put on "orange alert" and the French navy deployed three rescue vessels to be on stand by in case of maritime accidents.

(http://www.telegraph.co.uk/news/worldnews/europe/france/4580079/French-storms-leave-half-a-million-without-electricity.html)

11. Ladies and gentlemen, _____ has the global community been under such stress. The ties that bind us, as humankind, are fraying. We must work especially hard to preserve them, at this critical juncture, in the interests of our common future. Thank you very much and I will be happy to answer your questions. —Ban Ki Moon

(http://unic.org.in/display.php?E=1068&K=Press_Conference)

12. The potato has also given traders like Amina Nakate a business edge. At her stall in Nylon market, Mbale, time passes quickly for Nakate. _____ has she served a customer than another falls in line. In her 10 years of trading there, none of her products—like plantain and cassava—have sold as fast as the sweet potato, she said. In a day, she can sell about five 200kg bags of the product, yielding an income of 700,000 shillings ($208) per day—compared to $50 previously.

(http://www.braced.org/news/i/?id=d7a1eaab-3dcf-4488-b1f2-4a8030777228)

13. If you are happy to be contacted by a BBC journalist please leave a telephone number that we can contact you on. In some cases a selection of your comments will be published, displaying your name as you provide it and location, unless you state otherwise. Your contact details will never be published. When sending us pictures, video or eyewitness accounts _____ should you endanger yourself or others, take any unnecessary risks or infringe any laws. Please ensure you have read the terms and conditions.

(http://www.bbc.com/news/world-europe-36483045)

14. In the beginning, there were no searing head winds, but after the Hawi turnaround, all that changed. The relentless cross winds hit at 35 mph. The tall grass bent over backward and told me this was going to take a while. I needed to be patient, not become agitated or frustrated. I signed up for this, right? After a few more hours battling the winds and extreme heat, _____ was I so happy to see an airport. Landmark! It was 10 miles to the end of this oven-like ride, 125 degrees from lava rocks and road, with vicious winds.

(http://www.cnn.com/2015/10/30/health/ironman-championship-final-hawaii/)

15. _____ did I know that exactly two months later, the largest scientific organization in the world and publisher of the leading academic journal *Science* would launch an initiative aimed at doing just that—move the conversation forward by telling Americans "What We Know." It boils down to three main points—97 percent of climate scientists agree that climate change is here and now, that this means we risk abrupt and irreversible changes to the climate, and the sooner we act, the lower the costs and risks we face.

(http://www.ecowatch.com/how-scientists-are-moving-climate-change-conversation-forward-1881880099.html)

My Bookshelf > My eLab > Exercises > Unit 14

Expression/Form	Examples
Emphatic Adverbs	
At no time	**At no time** <u>should residents leave</u> their homes during a tornado.
Hardly	**Hardly** <u>had the rain ended</u> when our home became flooded.
Little	**Little** <u>did we know</u> that the storm would last for three days.
Never	**Never** <u>have I been</u> so frightened as during that storm.
No sooner	**No sooner** <u>had the rain ended</u> than the heavy winds began.
Not once	**Not once** <u>did I panic</u> while I was inside my house.
Not only	**Not only** <u>were trees felled</u> by the winds, (but) local rivers also flooded.
Not since	**Not since** my childhood <u>have I lived through</u> such extreme weather.
Not until	**Not until** the weather settled <u>did life return</u> to normal.
Only after	**Only after** the weather settled <u>did life return</u> to normal.
On no account	**On no account** <u>should people leave</u> their homes during a tornado.
Rarely	**Rarely** <u>have I witnessed</u> such rain damage.
Seldom	**Seldom** <u>does so much rain fall</u> in one day.
So + adjective	**So heavy** <u>was the rain</u> that local rivers broke their banks.
Under no circumstances	**Under no circumstances** <u>should you approach</u> a fallen power line.
. . . Neither	People living away from the coast were not affected. **Neither** <u>were the people</u> living on higher land.
. . . Nor	People living away from the coast were not affected. **Nor** <u>were the people</u> living on higher land.
Inversion	
To be as main verb	a) <u>Climate change is</u> the result of both human activity and natural phenomena. b) **Not only** <u>is climate change</u> the result of human activity, it is also caused by natural phenomena.
Verbs with auxiliaries	a) <u>Pacific storms have become</u> so severe that evacuation of communities is now a regular occurrence. b) **So severe** <u>have Pacific storms become</u> that evacuation of communities is now a regular occurrence.
Other verbs	a) <u>El Niño rarely leaves</u> coastal Pacific communities unscathed. b) **Rarely** <u>does El Niño leave</u> coastal Pacific communities unscathed.
Within an independent clause that begins with *it is/was*: no inversion	It was **not until** the end of the storm that <u>people ventured</u> out of their shelters. It was **only after** coastal erosion affected communities that <u>action was taken</u>.
Use of *not only* without inversion (correlative conjunction *not only . . . but also*)	**Not only** <u>does El Niño damage</u> coastal communities, it also affects people living further inland. (inversion) *BUT* <u>El Niño affects</u> **not only** coastal communities **but also** people living further inland. (no inversion) **Not only** <u>coastal communities</u> **but also** <u>people living further inland suffer</u> during El Niño years. (no inversion)

LINKING WORDS IN ACADEMIC WRITING

Linking words in academic writing connect ideas and add cohesion. In doing so, they make it easier for readers to understand the interrelationships between ideas, for example, emphasis, addition, cause and effect, and contrast.

In this appendix, you will study five groups of linking words:

- conjunctive adverbs
- coordinators
- subordinators
- correlative conjunctions
- other linking words and phrases

CONJUNCTIVE ADVERBS

Conjunctive adverbs are used to join ideas and arguments in different clauses and sentences. The conjunctive adverb you choose to use gives an indication to your reader of how you think your ideas are related. Conjunctive adverbs can be placed at the beginning of independent clauses, in the middle, or at the end.

Meaning

Conjunctive adverbs convey a range of meanings, most commonly:

- addition: *moreover, in addition*
- contrast: *however, nonetheless*
- result: *therefore, consequently*

> The Mediterranean diet has been linked to reduced rates of heart disease**; moreover,** it may also reduce cancer rates. (addition)
>
> Many doctors recommend olive oil**; however,** it is more expensive than other oils used for cooking. (contrast)
>
> The Mediterranean diet is low in unhealthy fats**; therefore,** it may reduce cholesterol. (result)

Conjunctive adverbs and adverbial phrases are also used for other functions, including the following:

- introducing: *to begin with, first(ly)*
- summarizing: *in brief, in short, to summarize, to sum up*
- concluding: *in conclusion, to conclude*

Conjunctive Adverbs That Refer to a Previous Idea

Certain conjunctive adverbs are used specifically to connect the second part of a sentence, or a new sentence, to an idea stated previously. The conjunctive adverb may show contrast with the previous idea (*in contrast, on the other hand*), contradict or challenge it (*instead, on the contrary*), or restate it, with or without expanding on it (*in other words, specifically*).

Accuracy and Punctuation

Use conjunctive adverbs between, within, or after independent clauses. If the conjunctive adverb is placed between two independent clauses, set it off with a period or semicolon, and a comma. If it is placed within an independent clause, set it off with commas.

Between Independent Clauses

The Mediterranean diet has been linked to reduced rates of heart disease**. Moreover,** it may also reduce cancer rates. (with a period and comma)

The Mediterranean diet has been linked to reduced rates of heart disease**; moreover,** it may also reduce cancer rates. (with a semicolon and comma)

Within an Independent Clause

Some doctors**, however,** believe the health benefits are overstated. (with commas)

After an Independent Clause

Some doctors believe the health benefits are overstated**, however.** (with a comma and period)

Style

Conjunctive adverbs add a sense of formality to your writing. However, if you begin too many successive independent clauses with conjunctive adverbs, your writing may lack flow and appear formulaic. If this is the case, consider combining conjunctive adverbs with alternatives. Compare the following two paragraphs:

The Mediterranean diet has been linked to reduced rates of heart disease**; moreover,** it may also reduce cancer rates. **As a result,** many doctors recommend olive oil**. However,** olive oil is unaffordable for many people**. Therefore,** nutritionists should suggest cheaper alternatives. (formulaic and lacking in flow)

The Mediterranean diet, which has been linked to reduced rates of heart disease, may also reduce cancer rates. Many doctors are, therefore, recommending olive oil. Because olive oil is unaffordable for many people, nutritionists should also suggest cheaper alternatives. (rewritten for more variety and better flow)

Some writers would not set off *therefore* with commas in the second example because they feel the commas break the flow of the sentence.

Summary: Conjunctive Adverbs and Adverbial Phrases

Conjunctive Adverbs	Use	Examples
Addition		
additionally furthermore in addition moreover	To add ideas	Olive oil is high in monounsaturated fats**; additionally / furthermore / in addition / moreover,** it contains polyphenols, which may prevent heart disease.
equally likewise similarly	To express similarity	Olive oil is widely used in salads. **Equally/ Likewise/Similarly,** grapeseed oil is a healthy option for salads and mayonnaise.
in other words specifically	To restate, or expand on, a previously stated idea	Foods high in sugar and saturated fat are linked to poor health**; in other words,** people should avoid them. Foods high in sugar and saturated fat are linked to poor health, **specifically,** obesity and heart disease.
Contrast		
however nevertheless nonetheless still	To express contrast	Olive oil is a healthy option. **However/ Nevertheless/Nonetheless/Still,** it is too expensive for many families to use regularly.
as opposed to in contrast on the other hand	To express contrast with a previously stated idea	Processed food is often unhealthy **as opposed to** homemade meals, which tend to contain less sugar, salt, and fat. Processed food with high levels of sugar, salt, and fat should be avoided. **In contrast / On the other hand,** homemade alternatives can offer a balanced and healthy diet.
instead on the contrary rather	To contradict or challenge a previously stated idea	I was told if I followed the new diet, I would gain energy. On the contrary, it made me feel weaker.
Result		
as a result consequently therefore thus	To describe results or effects	The Mediterranean diet may help prevent heart disease. **As a result / Consequently / Therefore / Thus,** it has gained in popularity.

Note that *in other words* is set off by a semicolon and a comma because it precedes an independent clause, but *specifically* is set off by commas because it is placed within the independent clause.

Coordinators are used for two main purposes: to link two or more independent clauses and to join items in a series or list. There are seven coordinators, known as the "FANBOYS": *For*, *And*, *Nor*, *But*, *Or*, *Yet*, *So*.

Meaning

When you link two ideas with a coordinator, it is important to consider the relationship between the two ideas and to select the coordinator that best conveys your intended meaning. The FANBOYS coordinators convey the following meanings:

- addition (including alternatives): *and, nor, or*
- contrast: *but, yet*
- cause and effect: *for, so*

> The final exam was yesterday, **and** 80 students were present. (addition)
>
> The exam was difficult, **but** some students still got high grades. (contrast)
>
> I knew the exam would be difficult, **so** I prepared for two weeks. (result)

Emphasis

To review compound sentences, see Unit 3, p. 18.

If a writer joins independent clauses with a coordinator, they form a compound sentence. Generally speaking, compound sentences give equal emphasis to the ideas in each independent clause, as in the following example:

> Students can take the exam in person, **or** they can choose to do it online.

Accuracy and Punctuation

Use coordinators to join independent clauses. In North American varieties of English, it is normal to place a comma before the coordinator; in British and other varieties of English, no comma is required.

> I had no time to prepare for the exam, **yet** I still got an A. (with comma)
>
> I had no time to prepare for the exam **yet** I still got an A. (no comma)

Style

If you use too may compound sentences, your writing style may seem rather simple and repetitive. If the relationship between two independent clauses is cause and effect or contrast, you may want to consider alternatives with different structures, for example:

I knew the final exam would be difficult, **so** I prepared for two weeks.	(compound sentence with the coordinator *so*)
I knew the final exam would be difficult; **therefore,** I prepared for two weeks.	(two independent clauses joined by the conjunctive adverb *therefore*)
Since I knew the final exam would be difficult, I prepared for two weeks.	(complex sentence formed with the subordinator *since*)

Summary: Coordinators

For has a literary, narrative tone; it is uncommon in most academic writing.

When *nor* is placed at the beginning of an independent clause, invert the subject-verb order (see Unit 14, p. 93).

Coordinator	Use	Example
for	To express a reason	My school years were happy, **for** I had not a care in the world.
and	To add information and examples	The final exam took place yesterday, **and** 80 students were present in the exam hall.
nor	To add information and examples in negative sentences	Students could not check their notes, **nor** were they allowed to use calculators.
but	To join ideas when there is an idea of contrast	The final exam was difficult, **but** some students still got high grades.
or	To add alternative information and examples	Students can take the exam in person, **or** they can choose to do it online.
yet	To express an unexpected idea of contrast	I had no time to prepare for the exam, **yet** I still managed to get an A.
so	To express an effect or result	I knew the final exam would be difficult, **so** I prepared for two weeks.
In Series or Lists		
and	To add a similar item to a series or list	To prepare for the writing test, I revised articles, tenses, **and** punctuation.
or	To add an alternative item to a series or list	I had three choices: retake the course, retake the final exam, **or** accept the N (incomplete) grade.

SUBORDINATORS

To review dependent clauses and complex sentences, see Unit 3, pp. 17 and 18.

Subordinators can be used to link the ideas in two clauses. When subordinators are used at the beginning of a clause, they make it dependent. The dependent clause (also called a *subordinate clause*) should be joined to an independent clause to make a complete, complex sentence.

Meaning

When you link two clauses with a subordinator, you can convey a range of meanings about how the two clauses interrelate:

- time: *before, while*
- contrast: *although, whereas*
- reason: *because, since*
- condition: *if, whether*

Before nuclear power was developed, most power stations were coal-fired. (time)

Although nuclear power is efficient, it does present serious risks. (contrast)

Many people oppose nuclear power **because** they worry about accidents. (reason)

Some climate change activists are unsure **whether** the risks outweigh the benefits. (condition)

Emphasis

Complex sentences are often written with a dependent clause preceding the independent clause. In such cases, the information in the independent clause usually carries more emphasis. If the independent clause precedes the dependent clause, the emphasis is less clear.

1. **Although** nuclear power is efficient, it does present serious risks.
2. Many people oppose nuclear power **because** they worry about accidents.

In sentence 1, the idea of serious risk is emphasized as the independent clause comes second in the sentence. In sentence 2, the dependent clause comes second in the sentence; in this case, it is less clear whether the writer is emphasizing opposition or accidents.

Accuracy and Punctuation

Use a comma to separate dependent and independent clauses if the dependent clause comes first in the sentence. No comma is required if the dependent clause comes second in the sentence.

> **Although** nuclear power is efficient**,** it does present serious risks. (with comma)

> Many people oppose nuclear power **because** they worry about accidents. (no comma)

Style

The use of subordinators and complex sentences adds a degree of formality and sophistication to academic writing. This is especially the case when two clauses are related by an idea of time, contrast, or cause and effect.

> Most power stations used to be coal-fired; **then** nuclear energy was developed.

> **Before** nuclear power was developed, most power stations were coal-fired. (improved academic style)

> Nuclear power is efficient, **but** it does present serious risks.

> **Although** nuclear power is efficient, it does present serious risks. (added formality)

> Many people oppose nuclear power, **and** they worry about accidents. (imprecise expression of cause and effect)

> Many people oppose nuclear power **because** they worry about accidents. (improved academic style)

Summary: Subordinators

Subordinators	Use	Examples
Time		
after *as long as* *as soon as* *before* *until* *when* *while*	To convey time relations	**Before** nuclear power was developed, most power stations were coal-fired. **After** an earthquake caused a nuclear meltdown at a nearby power plant, public confidence in nuclear power declined. **When** the site for the power station was announced, local people expressed concern about health risks. **While** the site was being developed, the environment protection agency carried out a detailed assessment. Construction began **as soon as** the assessment was complete. **As long as** people need electricity, nuclear power will have a place in the energy market. The plant didn't open **until** all safety checks had been made.
Contrast		
although *even though* *whereas* *while* *whilst* (British English)	To express contrast	**Although** nuclear power is efficient, it does present serious risks. The project was completed **even though** it ran over budget by $20 million. (stronger contrast than *although*) The previous power plant took several years to build **whereas/while/whilst** it replacement was finished in five.
Reason		
because *as* *since*	To describe reasons	Many people oppose nuclear power **because/as/since** they worry about accidents.
Condition		
if *unless* *whether*	To describe conditions	**If** nuclear power reduces global CO_2 emissions, should it be supported in the fight against climate change? **Unless** the risks are reduced, many people may remain suspicious of nuclear energy. Environmentalists are divided over **whether** they should support nuclear power. (two possibilities)

As and *since* can also convey time relations, so avoid using them to describe reasons unless the meaning is clear.

Correlative conjunctions are linking words that are used in pairs to join two or more related ideas in a sentence.

Meaning

Correlative conjunctions can be used to express the following meanings, often with a sense of emphasis:

- addition: *both . . . and, not only . . . (but) also*
- one or the other: *either . . . or, neither . . . nor, whether . . . or*

> **Both** English **and** Mandarin are major world languages. (addition)
>
> **Neither** English **nor** Spanish majors can take the course. (not one or the other)

Accuracy

If a sentence contains two subjects joined by a pair of correlative conjunctions, the verb agrees with the nearer subject.

To review subject-verb agreement and parallel structure, see Units 10 and 12, pp. 65 and 79.

> **Neither** Mandarin classes **nor** individual instruction **is offered** at the university.
>
> **Either** Advanced English **or** elective foreign language courses **are taken** in the second year.

Maintain parallel structure when using correlative conjunctions.

> English majors can study **not only** English literature **but also** linguistics.
>
> English majors can complete their programs by **either** studying linguistics **or** taking elective foreign language courses.

Style

Correlative conjunctions add a formal, academic style to writing.

Summary: Correlative Conjunctions

Correlative Conjunctions	Use	Examples
Addition		
both . . . and *not only . . . (but) also*	To add ideas and examples	**Both** English **and** Mandarin are major world languages. Mandarin is **not only** difficult to pronounce, **but** it is **also** hard to write.
One or the Other		
either . . . or *neither . . . nor* *whether . . . or*	To express the idea of one or the other	English majors can take **either** 19th century poetry **or** modern fiction. **Neither** French **nor** Spanish majors can take the course. **Whether** you take Spanish **or** choose another elective, the courses will be for four credits.

The following are additional linking words and phrases that are common in academic writing.

Linking Words for Exemplification

A specific group of conjunctive adverbs is used to introduce examples in sentences:

- *for example*
- *for instance*
- *namely*
- *such as*

1. College writing poses many challenges**, for example,** when students have to learn and use different citation styles.
2. College writing poses many challenges**, for instance,** academic vocabulary and correct citation style.
3. College writing is challenging**; for example,** students need to use formal English and correct citation style.

In sentence 1, *for example* is set off by commas because the following example is a dependent clause. In sentence 2, *for instance* is set off by commas because the following examples are noun phrases. In sentence 3, *for example* is set off by a semicolon and a comma because the following example is an independent clause.

4. Citation styles **such as** APA and MLA are challenging.
5. Most college essays**, such as** lab reports and response papers**,** require specific structures.

In sentence 4, *such as* introduces a defining phrase, so no commas are required. In sentence 5, *such as* introduces a non-defining phrase, so commas are required.

6. Good college writing is based on two key skills**, namely,** effective reading and critical thinking.
7. Good college writers use two key skills**; namely,** they read effectively and think critically.

In sentence 6, *namely* is set off by commas because the following examples are noun phrases. In sentence 7, *namely* is set off by a semicolon and a comma because the following example is an independent clause.

Linking Words for Enumeration

Another type of conjunctive adverb is commonly used to add cohesion in academic writing by expressing sequence:

- *first(ly)*
- *second(ly)*
- *third(ly)*
- *finally*

College writing poses several challenges to first-year students. **First,** it is often very different from the writing they did in secondary school. **Second,** students have to learn how to write many different types of essay. **Third,** they often get less support from their instructors. **Finally,** the stakes are much higher.

35 MISTAKES TO AVOID IN ACADEMIC WRITING

A complete list of mistakes to avoid in academic writing would be endless. Here are 35 common mistakes that writers make.

PUNCTUATION

The following are common mistakes when using commas, semicolons, and colons.

1. Comma Splices

Avoid writing comma splices: sentences in which two independent clauses are joined by a comma.

- ✗ Crime prevention strategies have been successful during the last year**,** they also have the support of the central government.
- ✓ Crime prevention strategies have been successful during the last year**;** they also have the support of the central government.
- ✓ Crime prevention strategies have been successful during the last year**.** They also have the support of the central government.

2. Commas: Inconsistency

It is important to use commas consistently. For example, you should avoid including commas in some sentences and not in others (e.g., before coordinators and after introductory phrases—in bold in the following examples).

- ✗ **Between 2002 and 2012** crime fell gradually within the European Union. **During the same period,** violent crime fell in some EU countries **yet** figures rose in others. The inconsistency in violent crime rates is difficult to explain**, and** criminologists are looking for explanations.
- ✓ **Between 2002 and 2012,** crime fell gradually within the European Union. **During the same period,** violent crime fell in some EU countries**, yet** figures rose in others. The inconsistency in violent crime rates is difficult to explain**, and** criminologists are looking for explanations.

3. Commas: Confusing Sentences

In several writing genres, for example, journalistic and informal writing, commas are not used consistently after introductory phrases before an independent clause. If you are not including commas after introductory phrases, avoid confusing your reader due to the lack of commas.

- ✗ To reduce **crime prevention** is a more effective focus than punishment.
- ✓ To reduce **crime, prevention** is a more effective focus than punishment.

Because *crime prevention* is a common compound noun, if the writer omits the comma, the first part of the sentence could be read as "to reduce crime prevention" rather than "to reduce crime."

4. Semicolons: Incorrect Use in Complex Sentences

It is incorrect to use a semicolon to separate a dependent and independent clause in a complex sentence. Use a comma instead.

- ✗ Although the fair trade movement benefits many small-scale farmers worldwide**;** it benefits intermediaries even more.
- ✓ Although the fair trade movement benefits many small-scale farmers worldwide**,** it benefits intermediaries even more.

5. Semicolons: Incorrect Use in Lists of Items

Use semicolons to separate items in a list only if at least one of the items includes a comma.

- ✗ The fair trade movement needs to find strategies to address three important issues: expensive registration costs**;** excessive profits for intermediaries**;** and unstable product prices in world markets.
- ✓ The fair trade movement needs to find strategies to address three important issues: expensive registration costs**,** excessive profits for intermediaries**,** and unstable product prices in world markets.
- ✓ The fair trade movement needs to find strategies to address three important issues: expensive registration costs**,** which affect farmers**;** excessive profits for intermediaries**;** and unstable product prices in world markets.

6. Colons: Incorrect Use When Introducing Examples and Lists

Do not use a colon when you introduce a list or examples that are incorporated grammatically into the sentence.

- ✗ Two key challenges in international business relations in Africa are**:** responding to globalization and adapting to Western business practices.
- ✓ Two key challenges in international business relations in Africa are responding to globalization and adapting to Western business practices.
- ✓ Two key challenges in international business relations in Africa are **the following:** responding to globalization and adapting to Western business practices.
- ✓ Business leaders in Africa face two key **challenges:** responding to globalization and adapting to Western business practices.

7. Colons: Incorrect Use When Introducing Direct Quotations

It is correct usage to place a colon at the end of an independent clause to introduce direct quotations. However, do not use a colon to introduce a direct quotation that is incorporated grammatically into the sentence.

- ✗ It is important for leadership assessments to be performed**:** "in a structured manner, primarily based on behavioral criteria" (Peus et al., 2012, p. 106).

✓ It is important for leadership assessments to be performed "in a structured manner, primarily based on behavioral criteria" (Peus et al., 2012, p. 106).

✓ Leadership assessments should be performed to link organizational structure and work patterns **as follows:** "in a structured manner, primarily based on behavioral criteria" (Peus et al., 2012, p. 106).

LINKING WORDS

Avoid the following mistakes when you use linking words to join your ideas and arguments.

8. *Although* and *Even Though* Followed Directly by a Comma

Do not introduce a sentence with the subordinators *although* or *even though* followed by a comma.

✗ Certain nutritionists recommend olive oil. **Although,** it is too expensive for many families to use on a daily basis.

✓ Certain nutritionists recommend olive oil. **However,** it is too expensive for many families to use on a daily basis. (Use a conjunctive adverb such as *however*.)

✓ **Although** certain nutritionists recommend olive oil, it is too expensive for many families to use on a daily basis. (Move the subordinator to form a dependent clause.)

9. *Although* and *Even Though* with *But*

This is a common mistake when translating from certain languages into English.

If you begin a dependent clause with *although* or *even though*, do not begin the following independent clause with *but*. The idea of contrast has already been expressed by the subordinator.

✗ Although certain nutritionists recommend olive oil, **but** it is too expensive for many families to use on a daily basis.

✓ Although certain nutritionists recommend olive oil, it is too expensive for many families to use on a daily basis.

10. *In Contrast* versus *On the Contrary*

Use *in contrast* to introduce contrasting information. Use *on the contrary* to contradict or disagree with an argument stated previously.

✗ High school writing often involves formulas such as the five-paragraph essay. **On the contrary,** college writing varies greatly across the disciplines.

✓ High school writing often involves formulas such as the five-paragraph essay. **In contrast,** college writing varies greatly across the disciplines.

✓ It has been argued that high school writing is too easy. **On the contrary,** I found that many students wrote a range of challenging texts in Grades 11 and 12.

Avoid the following mistakes with nouns and verbs commonly used in academic writing.

11. *Criteria* and *Phenomena*: Singular versus Plural Forms

Nouns that have their origins in Greek, for example, *criteria* and *phenomena*, are often used incorrectly, even by experienced academics. Avoid confusing the singular and plural forms of these nouns.

   ✗ The criteria for the in-class essay **was** confusing.

   ✓ The criteria for the in-class essay **were** confusing.

   ✗ There are many important **criterion** for college success.

   ✓ There are many important **criteria** for college success.

   ✗ The essay was about a weather **phenomena** known as *urban heat islands*.

   ✓ The essay was about a weather **phenomenon** known as *urban heat islands*.

   ✗ Several **phenomenon** cause urban heat islands.

   ✓ Several **phenomena** cause urban heat islands.

12. *Effect* versus *Affect*

Avoid making mistakes with *effect* and *affect* when describing causal relations. Each word can be used as a noun or a verb with different meanings. In most contexts, *effect* is a noun and *affect*, the corresponding verb, as illustrated below.

   ✗ Higher temperatures and pollution had a negative **affect** on air quality in the city.

   ✓ Higher temperatures and pollution had a negative **effect** on air quality in the city. (noun)

   ✗ Higher temperatures and pollution **effected** air quality in the city.

   ✓ Higher temperatures and pollution **affected** air quality in the city. (verb)

Effect can also be used as a verb meaning "to bring something about or make happen." *Affect* as a noun refers to emotional impact. The following examples illustrate these less common usages.

   ✓ The new anti-pollution policies **effected** little change in the city.

   ✓ **Affect** is an important psychological factor in individuals' responses to requests and instructions.

13. *Affect* versus *Effect on, Emphasize* versus *Emphasis on*

In several cases, when you have the choice of expressing relationships of cause and effect or emphasis with either a verb or a corresponding noun, use the preposition *on* with the noun.

   ✗ Higher temperatures and pollution **affected on** air quality in the city.

   ✓ Higher temperatures and pollution **affected** air quality in the city.

   ✓ Higher temperatures and pollution **had an effect on** air quality in the city.

✗ The new mayor **emphasized on** tackling air pollution when he came to office.

✓ The new mayor **emphasized** tackling air pollution when he came to office.

✓ The new mayor **placed an emphasis on** tackling air pollution when he came to office.

HOMOPHONES

Some words sound the same but have different meanings and spellings. The following examples are commonly confused.

14. *There, Their,* and *They're*

✗ **Their** are several benefits to using cellphones for learning.

✓ **There** are several benefits to using cellphones for learning.

✗ Many teachers don't allow students to use cellphones in **there** classes.

✓ Many teachers don't allow students to use cellphones in **their** classes.

✗ Students may distract others when **there** texting friends.

✓ Students may distract others when **they're** texting friends.

15. *Your* and *You're*

✗ Please check **you're** phone for updates to the schedule.

✓ Please check **your** phone for updates to the schedule.

✗ **Your** arriving at 11:45 tomorrow morning.

✓ **You're** arriving at 11:45 tomorrow afternoon.

SPELLING: DOUBLE CONSONANTS

16. Incorrect Double Consonants

Writers sometimes make mistakes when they are spelling multi-syllable words that may or may not require double consonants when adding a suffix. If the suffix begins with a vowel (*ed, ing*), you can often apply the following rule: a) double the consonant after *a short stressed vowel sound*; b) do not double the consonant after *an unstressed vowel sound*.

✗ The artefacts were **intered** 2,000 years ago.

✓ The artefacts were **interred** 2,000 years ago.

✗ The archaeologists **enterred** the site after a year of preparation.

✓ The archaeologists **entered** the site after a year of preparation.

RELATIVE CLAUSES

The following are some of the most common mistakes that writers make when they form relative clauses.

17. Confusing Defining and Non-Defining Relative Clauses

Avoid writing non-defining relative clauses as defining relative clauses, and vice versa.

In each example below, the defining relative clause gives essential information about the subject of the independent clause. It explains that the writer is referring to a specific Business class—the one she is taking this term, not the other Business classes she may have taken. Do not set off defining clauses with commas, and use the relative pronouns *that* or *which* for things.

    ✗ The Business class**, that I'm taking this term,** is difficult.

    ✓ The Business class **that I'm taking this term** is difficult.

    ✓ The Business class **which I'm taking this term** is difficult. (British English)

In the next two examples, the non-defining clause gives non-essential information about the noun *exam* in the independent clause. It provides extra information— that the Business exam was more difficult than expected. Set off non-defining clauses with commas, and use the relative pronoun *which* for things, not *that*. Note that the incorrect non-defining clause suggests that there was more than one exam: one that was more difficult than expected and one that wasn't.

    ✗ I got an A in the Business exam **which was more difficult than expected**.

    ✓ I got an A in the Business exam**, which was more difficult than expected**.

18. *That* versus *Where*

Avoid incorrect use of *that* and *where* in defining relative clauses that require a verb and corresponding preposition. The following examples show incorrect and correct usage of *that* and *where* in phrases that refer to the following idea: I lived in that country when I was a child.

    ✗ That is the country **that I lived** when I was a child. (The preposition *in* is missing.)

    ✗ That is the country **where I lived in** when I was a child. (The preposition *in* is unnecessary.)

    ✓ That is the country **that I lived in** when I was a child.

    ✓ That is the country **where I lived** when I was a child.

    ✓ That is the country **in which I lived** when I was a child. (formal)

19. *Whom* versus *Who*: Direct Objects

Whom can be used when referring to a person who is the direct object of the relative clause.

    ✗ He's the teaching assistant **whom** taught the lab class last term.

    ✓ He's the teaching assistant **who** taught the lab class last term.

    ✓ Is he the teaching assistant **whom** you recommended?

The first sentence is incorrect because *whom* should be *who* (as in sentence 2); it is the subject of the relative clause, referring back to *he*: *He taught the lab class last term*. The third sentence is correct because *whom* is the object of the relative clause, replacing *him*: *You recommended **him***.

20. *Whom* versus *Who*: After Prepositions

Whom should also be used after prepositions.

    ✗ She's the student with **who** you took the lab class last term.

    ✓ She's the student with **whom** you took the lab class last term.

DANGLING MODIFIERS

Dangling modifiers are phrases or clauses, usually at the beginning of sentences, that "dangle"—in other words, they do not correspond to the grammatical subject of the main clause.

21. Dangling Modifiers: Participle Phrases

Dangling modifiers are most common in sentences that begin with participle phrases.

    ✗ **Originating in the 1980s,** I became interested in the slow food movement.

    ✓ **Originating in the 1980s,** slow food emerged in response to the spread of fast food.

    ✗ **Launched in 2001,** they soon learned about Slow Food International.

    ✓ **Launched in 2001,** Slow Food International gained worldwide attention.

The first incorrect sentence can be read as meaning the writer originated in the 1980s, not the slow food movement. The second incorrect sentence reads as if "they" were launched in 2001.

22. Dangling Modifiers: Preposition Phrases

In addition, avoid dangling modifiers in sentences that begin with preposition phrases.

    ✗ **At the age of 25,** the slow food movement became an integral part of my life.

    ✓ **At the age of 25,** I became very involved in the slow food movement.

PRONOUNS

Pronouns are words that take the place of a noun or noun phrase. For example, in the following sentence, the pronoun *him* refers to the noun *Michael*.

    I bumped into Michael and asked **him** if I could borrow his lecture notes.

23. *I* versus *Me*

Use *and I* if a verb follows immediately. Use *and me* if no verb follows.

    ✗ **You and me** should attend the lecture next week.

    ✓ **You and I** should attend the lecture next week.

    ✗ She lent her lecture notes to **you and I**.

    ✓ She lent her lecture notes to **you and me**.

24. Ambiguous Pronouns

Avoid using pronouns that may confuse your reader by referring to more than one noun. In the following sentence, it is not clear whether the classmates or the lecture notes are not helpful.

✗ My classmates rarely share lecture notes because **they** aren't very helpful.

✓ My classmates rarely share lecture notes because they are too competitive.

✓ My classmates rarely share lecture notes because the notes they take aren't very helpful.

DESCRIBING QUANTITY

Be careful not to make mistakes with quantifiers such as *some*, and with phrases such as *a large number of* and a *large amount of.*

25. *Some* versus *Some of*

Use *some of* before determiners such as *the, those, my,* etc. The same rule applies for other quantifiers, for example, *many, a few,* etc.

✗ **Some of** questions in the quiz were very difficult.

✓ **Some** questions in the quiz were very difficult.

✓ **Some of the** questions in the quiz were very difficult.

26. *A Large Amount of* versus *A Large Number of*

Use *a large amount of* with uncountable nouns (nouns that have no plural form). Use *a large number of* with plural countable nouns.

✗ **A large amount of** students dislike final exams.

✓ **A large number of** students dislike final exams.

✓ There was **a large amount of** confusion about the final exam format.

27. *Less* versus *Fewer*

Use *less* with uncountable nouns and *fewer* with countable nouns. Avoid the common mistake of using *less* with plural countable nouns.

✗ The final exam had **less problem-solving questions** than the mid-term test.

✓ The final exam had **fewer problem-solving questions** than the mid-term test.

28. *Little, A Little, Few,* and *A Few*

Before uncountable nouns, *little* means "virtually none" while *a little* means "a small amount."

I had **little difficulty** answering all the questions. (virtually no difficulty)

I had **a little difficulty** answering all the questions. (a small amount of difficulty)

Before plural countable nouns, *few* means "virtually none" while *a few* means "a small number." *Little* means "small" when used with countable nouns.

> There were **few questions** that I couldn't answer. (virtually no questions)
>
> There were **a few questions** that I couldn't answer. (a small number of questions)
>
> I had **a little problem** with the final question. (small, not serious problem)

> ✗ There were **little questions** that I couldn't answer. (This means the questions were physically small.)
> ✓ There were **few questions** that I couldn't answer.

> ✗ I hope there are **few questions** that I will be able to answer. (This means the speaker does not want to be able to answer the questions!)
> ✓ I hope there are **a few questions** that I will be able to answer.

IN-TEXT CITATIONS AND REFERENCE LISTS

The following are seven common mistakes to avoid when citing sources and writing reference list entries.

29. Reference List Not in Alphabetical Order

It is a requirement for APA and MLA citation styles that reference list entries be ordered alphabetically by author's surname (or by publishing organization, or title for works with no identifiable author). Occasionally, titles of a work begin with a number; such works should be ordered numerically, coming before titles beginning with a letter. The following examples of an APA reference list illustrate this point.

> ✗ Casanave, C. P. (2002). *Writing games: Multicultural case studies of academic literacy practices in higher education*. Mahwah, NJ: Lawrence Erlbaum Associates.
>
> Bailey, C., & Challen, R. (2015). Student perceptions of the value of Turnitin text-matching software as a learning tool. *Practitioner Research in Higher Education*, *9*(1), 38–51.
>
> European Environment Agency. (2016). *Explaining road transport emissions: A non-technical guide*. Copenhagen: EEA.

> ✓ 3D printing. (2016, January 26). In *Encyclopædia Britannica*. Retrieved from https://www.britannica.com/technology/3D-printing
>
> Bailey, C., & Challen, R. (2015). Student perceptions of the value of Turnitin text-matching software as a learning tool. *Practitioner Research in Higher Education*, *9*(1), 38–51.
>
> Casanave, C. P. (2002). *Writing games: Multicultural case studies of academic literacy practices in higher education*. Mahwah, NJ: Lawrence Erlbaum Associates.
>
> European Environment Agency. (2016). *Explaining road transport emissions: A non-technical guide*. Copenhagen: EEA.

30. No Corresponding Reference List Entry for an In-Text Citation

Every in-text citation in the main body of the essay requires a corresponding entry in the reference list (except personal communications in APA style). Always cross-reference each in-text citation to avoid this mistake.

31. No Corresponding In-Text Citation for a Reference List Entry

Every reference list entry should correspond with an in-text citation in the main body of the essay. Always cross-reference each reference list entry to avoid this mistake.

32. Mismatch between the In-Text Citation and Reference List Entry

A reference list entry should begin with the same surname, organization, or work title as is indicated parenthetically in the corresponding in-text citation. Avoid a mismatch between the two as illustrated below.

> **In-text citation:** ("3D printing," 2016)
> **References**

> ✗ *Encyclopædia Britannica*. (2016, January 26). 3D printing. Retrieved from https://www.britannica.com/technology/3D-printing

> ✓ 3D printing. (2016, January 26). In *Encyclopædia Britannica*. Retrieved from https://www.britannica.com/technology/3D-printing

33. Formatting Inconsistencies

Avoid mixing up different citation styles as the following example illustrates. APA style is in bold, and MLA style is underlined.

> ✗ Recent research has focused on different aspects of the business leadership nexus between China and the West: for example, how three leading Chinese philosophies—Daoism, Confucianism, and Legalism—can complement Western-influenced leadership in China **(Ma & Tsui, 2015)**, and the need for Chinese approaches to stem the shift of Chinese leaders toward Western practices (Li 1–2). **Kim and Moon (2015)** focus on leadership and Corporate Social Responsibility (CSR), comparing CSR in Asia (from Pakistan eastward to Japan) and Western CSR, while the determinants for success in business leadership and the role of women leaders in China, India, and Singapore are discussed in **Peus, Braun, and Knipfer (2015)**. A recent study has also highlighted the need to promote Indigenous African forms of knowledge to meet the needs of the African workforce, addressing the growth in Asia-Africa relations (Kamoche et al. 331).

34. Ungrammatical Incorporation of Quotations

All short direct quotations (fewer than 40 words in APA style or four lines in MLA style) should be incorporated grammatically into sentences. Use a colon before direct quotations only if the quotation does not flow grammatically in the sentence.

Original information: Drawing on articles that reported interviews of fifteen business leaders, we code their leadership behaviors according to the school they exemplify. We use these fifteen cases to illustrate, rather than as a test of, the propositions. Finally, we discuss how traditional culture could be a rich source of understanding for future leadership research in China and beyond. (Ma & Tsui, 2015, p. 14)

✗ Ma and Tsui (2015) present interviews with 15 Chinese business leaders in their analysis of traditional Chinese culture and its **potential "a** rich source of understanding for future leadership research" (p. 14).

✗ Ma and Tsui (2015) present interviews with 15 Chinese business leaders in their analysis of traditional Chinese culture and its **potential as: "a** rich source of understanding for future leadership research" (p. 14).

✓ Ma and Tsui (2015) present interviews with 15 Chinese business leaders in their analysis of traditional Chinese culture and its **potential as "a** rich source of understanding for future leadership research" (p. 14).

35. Lack of Concision in Quotations

Direct quotations should be concise and include only key ideas. Other information should be paraphrased.

Original information: Although learning reflects knowledge acquired from teachers and others, thinking reflects digesting and internalizing what is learned. Ideal students of Confucius would use self-reflection to rigorously identify their own faults and develop actions for self improvement in the pursuit of self-perfection. (Ma & Tsui, p. 16)

✗ Ma and Tsui (2015) suggest that even though "learning reflects knowledge acquired from teachers and others, thinking reflects digesting and internalizing what is learned," and that ideally, "students of Confucius would use self-reflection to rigorously identify their own faults and develop actions for self improvement in the pursuit of self-perfection" (p. 16).

✓ Ma and Tsui (2015) suggest that learning is a reflection of what is learned from teachers and others, and that thinking is a reflection of how knowledge is internalized. According to the authors, from a Confucian perspective, self-reflection should be employed by learners as part of the process of "self improvement in the pursuit of self-perfection" (p. 16).

IDENTIFYING TYPES OF WORDS

n. (noun or noun phrase) a word that identifies a class of things – *a sunny **day***

v. (verb) a word that shows an action or a state – *I **walked** in the park.*

adj. (adjective) a word that modifies a noun – *a **sunny** day*

adv. (adverb) a word that most commonly modifies (i) a verb or (ii) adjective

    (i) *I walked **slowly**.* (modifying a verb)

    (ii) *It was **incredibly** hot in the park.* (modifying an adjective)

TERMINOLOGY FOR GRAMMAR AND SENTENCE STRUCTURE

action verb (n.) a verb that expresses the idea of action, i.e., doing something

active voice (n.) a sentence in which the **subject** is doing the action, e.g., ***Shakespeare** wrote Romeo and Juliet.*

adjacent to (adj.) next to

ambiguous (adj.) having more than one possible interpretation

article (n.) a word that introduces a noun phrase, e.g., *a* (indefinite article) and *the* (definite article)

auxiliary verbs (n.) a verb such as *may, might, have,* used to form tenses

certainty (n.) being sure about something

characteristic (n.) a feature of someone or something

clause (n.) part of a sentence containing a subject and a verb

cohesion (n.) keeping together

comma splice (n.) an incorrect sentence in which two independent clauses are joined with a comma

complex sentence (n.) a sentence made up of at least one independent clause and one dependent clause

compound sentence (n.) a sentence made up of at least two independent clauses

conditional sentence (n.) a sentence in which the action (expressed in the main clause) can only occur under a certain condition (expressed in the *if* clause)

conjunctive adverb (n.) a linking word in that joins ideas in one or more independent clauses, e.g., *however, moreover, therefore*

countable noun (n.) a noun that has a plural form, e.g., *computers*

defining relative clause (n.) a clause that identifies or defines a preceding thing or person in a sentence using relative pronouns such as *that* (things), *who* (people), *where* (place), e.g., *This is the computer **that I bought last week**.*

dependent clause (n.) a clause that cannot stand alone as a sentence

direct quotation (n.) using someone's exact words

economical style (n.) using fewer words

enumeration (n.) ordering by number

exemplification (n.) giving examples

FANBOYS coordinators (n.) the following linking words: *for, and, nor, but, or, yet, so,* which form compound sentences when they join two or more independent clauses, e.g., *I opened the door, **and** he walked past me.*

formulaic (adj.) following a method, lacking originality

general noun phrase (n.) a noun phrase that refers to all members of a group or category, e.g., *laptop computers*

hypothetical (adj.) imagined or possible, not real

independent clause (n.) a clause that can stand alone as a sentence, and which has a subject and a corresponding verb, e.g., *I bought a new laptop last week.*

infinitive (n.) the base form of a verb, e.g., *(to) take, (to) give*

intention (future) (n.) referring to the future in terms of something that someone wants or plans to do

intransitive verbs (n.) verbs that do not require an object

inversion for emphasis (n.) changing the subject-verb order of a sentence if the sentence begins with a negative adverbial phrase or word such as *not only, hardly, never,* e.g., *Never had I experienced such bad weather.*

likelihood (n.) the chance of something happening (if it is certain, probable, or possible)

main clause (n.) a clause including a subject and a verb that can form a sentence

modal auxiliary verbs (n.) a verb used with another verb to express ideas like obligation, likelihood, willingness, e.g., *may, might, will, must*

non-defining relative clause (n.) a clause that adds extra, non-essential information about a preceding thing in a sentence, usually beginning with words such as *which, who, when*, e.g., *Last week I did the exam, **which was really hard**.*

object (n.) the thing in a sentence affected by the verb: e.g., *I kicked **the ball**.*

obligation (n.) being bound, or obliged, to do something due to a sense of duty or moral obligation

parallel structure (n.) using the same types of words in sentences, especially in lists, e.g., *The weather was **hot, humid,** and **uncomfortable**.* (3 adjectives)

passive voice (n.) a grammatical form in which the **object** of a sentence is placed in subject position
> active voice: *Shakespeare wrote **Romeo and Juliet**.* **(object)**
> passive voice: ***Romeo and Juliet** was written by Shakespeare.* (in subject position)

past participle (n.) a verb form that usually ends in ed used in perfect tenses and with the passive voice, e.g., *I have **answered** the question already.*

phrase (n.) a group of words that does not have a subject and corresponding verb, e.g., *in the middle of the night*

possessive apostrophe (n.) an apostrophe that is added to a word to show that something belongs to someone or something, e.g., *the manager's boss*

preposition (n.) a word that indicates ideas such as place, time, or position, e.g., *in, on, at, by, with*

present participle (n.) a verb that ends with *ing* used in the present continuous tense (*they are **studying***), as an adjective (*a **reading** lamp*), and in active voice relative clauses (*the person who was **talking** to the manager – the person **talking** to the manager*)

relative pronoun (n.) a word such as *which, that, who* used to introduce a relative clause

run on sentence (n.) a grammatically incorrect sentence made up of two independent clause without punctuation separating them, e.g., *I talked to the manager she asked me to wait a little longer.*

sentence fragment (n.) a grammatically incomplete sentence that may be (i) missing a key component such as a subject, or (ii) a dependent clause written as a sentence:
> (i) *Had to wait too long.*
> (ii) *Because I had to wait too long.*

specific noun phrase (n.) a noun phrase that refers to a specific member or members of a group or category, e.g., ***the computer(s)** in room 354*

spontaneous decision (n.) a decision made suddenly without planning

state verb (n.) a verb that expresses a state (such as states of being, emotion, senses) rather than an action, e.g., *that bag **belongs** to me*

subject-verb agreement (n.) when the verb in a sentence conjugates correctly with the subject, e.g., *that bag **belongs** to me* (correct), as opposed to *that bag **belong** to me* (incorrect).

subordinator (n.) a linking word such as *although, because, despite*, that makes a clause dependent, e.g., ***Although** I studied hard, I got a B- for the test.*

transitive verbs (n.) verbs that require an object

uncountable noun (n.) a noun that has no plural form, e.g., *The city suffers from chronic **air pollution**.*

VOCABULARY FOR THE THEMES

3D (adj.) three-dimensional

acknowledgment (n.) accepting or recognizing that something exists

absolve someone of something (v.) say someone is not guilty or responsible

agitated (adj.) nervous

airborne diesel particles (n.) minute particles from diesel fuel that are in the air

ammonia (n.) a kind of gas, used for cleaning when mixed with water

APA citation style (n.) the style for writing in-text citations and reference lists of the American Psychological Association

artificial additives (n.) chemicals added to products, especially food

autism (n.) a developmental condition affecting people's communication and social relationships

autonomous cars (n.) cars that can operate without a driver

criteria (n.) factors

binding commitments (n.) agreements that both sides must obey, often by law

business edge (n.) an advantage in business

carbon emissions (n.) the release of carbon dioxide into the air

carbon footprint (n.) the amount of carbon dioxide and other greenhouse gases produced by human activity

cardiovascular disease (n.) diseases of the heart and blood vessels

cassava (n.) a root vegetable

CEO (n.) Chief Executive Officer

challenging (adj.) difficult

comply with (v.) follow rules, standards, or guidelines

conditional offer (n.) an offer to a college or university that is conditional upon the students attaining certain grades

connotation (n.) a suggested meaning

conscientious consumers (n.) consumers making an effort to buy goods carefully

control group (n.) people in an experiment who do not receive the treatment being tested

convergence (n.) moving together or becoming similar

corporate social responsibility (CSR) (n.) a business model that involves recognition of the law, ethics, and social impacts

credit (for university) (n.) a unit used for courses that count toward graduation

critical juncture (n.) important moment in time or history

crossvergence (n.) creating unique value systems across different countries as a result of connecting business and social factors

cyclone (n.) a severe wind storm

delegates (n.) people chosen to represent a group

delegation (n.) a group of delegates

diaspora (n.) a group of people living away from their homeland

digital learning (n.) learning with technology or online

disadvantage (v.) limit others' success

dispel (v.) make something (e.g., a myth or belief) go away

dispute settlement mechanism (n.) a system to resolve conflict and disagreements

divergence (n.) separation or difference

double-blind control trial (n.) an experiment in which one group receives a treatment and a control group receives a placebo; neither the researchers nor those participating know who has received which

ethically (adv.) related to morality, right and wrong

fair trade (n.) a movement that helps farmers in developing countries and promotes sustainable practice

feasibility (n.) the likelihood that something can be done or achieved

fluctuating (adj.) going up and down

fossil fuels (n.) fuels formed from plant or animal remains over millions of years, e.g., oil, coal, and gas

fray (v.) come apart, unravel

from scratch (adv.) from the beginning

genre (n.) a type of text

globalization (n.) the process of global integration of societies and economies

hindrance (n.) a thing that makes it difficult for people to do something

homeopathy (n.) a treatment that involves treating a condition with minute amounts of the substance that causes the condition

human resources (n.) usually a department in a company dealing with recruitment, work benefits, and employment standards

hybrid vehicles (n.) vehicles typically with an engine that runs on both gasoline and an electric battery

IELTS (n.) International English Language Testing System

Indigenous languages (n.) languages of Aboriginal people

initiatives (n.) actions to solve a problem or deal with an issue

inmates (n.) prisoners

intercultural awareness (n.) awareness of your own and others' cultures

intermediaries (n.) people working as links in a business chain

intermittently (adv.) irregularly, stopping and starting

laudable (adj.) deserving praise

living wage (n.) a wage that allows workers to meet their basic needs in society

logo (n.) a symbol that identifies something

longitudinal (adj.) over an extended period of time

mammoth task (n.) a very big, challenging task

manually controlled cars (n.) cars controlled by people's hands

mediation (n.) intervention to solve a dispute or conflict

Mediterranean diet (n.) a diet originating in countries such as Greece, Italy, and Spain, with high consumption of olive oil, vegetables, and fruits

MLA citation style (n.) the style for writing in-text citations and lists of works cited of the Modern Languages Association

MMR vaccine (n.) the vaccine for measles, mumps, and rubella

niche (n.) a specialized area or market

nitrogen dioxide (n.) a chemical compound emitted into the air through burning fuel

non-discrimination (n.) treating all people equally

odorous (adj.) having a smell

offenders (n.) people who break the law

pay a premium (v.) pay above the regular price for something

pediatric (adj.) relating to children or young people

pesticides (n.) substances used to protect crops by controlling harmful insects and weeds

placebo effect (n.) improvement due to belief in a treatment rather than the treatment itself

plagiarism (n.) copying the ideas of others without acknowledgment and presenting them as your own

plantain (n.) a type of banana that requires cooking

potholes (n.) a natural underground cave formed by water

predecessor (n.) a thing or person that came before or did a job before

primarily (adv.) mainly

processed food (n.) food that is prepared for consumers, often with high levels of salt, sugar, and fats

punitive (adj.) focusing on punishment

ratify (v.) formally approve something

reactors (n.) an industrial apparatus, e.g., to create nuclear energy

rebrand (v.) give something a new corporate image

reciprocity (n.) providing equal benefits to each other

regulators (n.) groups or organizations ensuring that laws and rules are followed

rehabilitation (n.) helping someone to become (again) a useful person in society

relentless (adj.) without stopping or becoming weaker

renewable energy (n.) energy from renewable sources such as the sun, wind, and water

residential schools (n.) boarding schools for Indigenous children who were forcibly removed from their families

restorative justice (n.) a system of dealing with crime through mediation between victims and offenders

retrospective (adj.) looking back in time

searing (adj.) burning, powerful

secretariat (n.) the administrative department of a large government or political organization

siren (n.) alarm

slow food (n.) a movement promoting ethical eating; anti-fast food

socio-demographic (adj.) related to society and population

solar power (n.) energy derived from the sun

subside (v.) to return to a normal level, e.g., the water level in a river

surgical implants (n.) an artificial device used to replace body parts, e.g., hips, teeth

surplus (n.) an excessive amount of something

sustainable farming (n.) farming that is linked to local environments, plant and animal life, which will continue through generations

TA (n.) teaching assistant

technologically literate (adv. + adj.) knowledgeable of how to use different technologies

therapeutic (adj.) used to treat an illness

tornado (n.) a damaging wind storm

transcultural awareness (n.) awareness of more than one culture and how they relate to each other

transparency (n.) visibility and accountability to others

trigger (v.) to cause or make happen

undeterred (adj.) not prevented or dissuaded from doing something

vertebra (n.) a section of the spine

woolly mammoth (n.) an extinct animal related to the Asian elephant